THE NEW DAY OF CHRISTIANITY

CHESTER P. MICHAEL

The New Day

of

Christianity

HELICON

Baltimore - Dublin

Helicon Press, Inc.
1120 N. Calvert Street
Baltimore, Maryland 21202

Library of Congress Catalog Card Number 65-15042

Nihil Obstat: Carroll E. Satterfield
Censor Librorum

Imprimatur: ✠ Lawrence J. Shehan, D.D.
Archbishop of Baltimore
December 4, 1964

The *Nihil Obstat* and *Imprimatur* are official declarations that a book or pamphlet is free of doctrinal or moral error. No implication is contained therein that those who have granted the *Nihil Obstat* and *Imprimatur* agree with the opinions expressed.

PRINTED IN THE UNITED STATES OF AMERICA BY
GARAMOND/PRIDEMARK PRESS, BALTIMORE, MARYLAND

Contents

THE NEW DAY OF CHRISTIANITY

Introduction

This book was not written for beginners in the life of grace, nor was it written for those who already have reached the higher mansions of passive contemplation. Rather, it is for those who have some knowledge of both the ways of grace and the ways of nature. It is kerygmatic in its approach, making some use of the discoveries of depth psychology and Christian existentialism in so far as they apply to the knowledge and practice of our Christian faith. The two authors recommended as background reading for a better understanding of what is written, are Rev. John Hofinger, S.J., and Rev. Josef Goldbrunner.

An attempt has been made in this book to bring together grace and nature, showing the beautiful relationship of love that can and should exist between them. Because of our inheritance of sin, it is not easy to keep the delicate balance that must exist between these two sides of our life. However, our success and happiness depend upon how well we do succeed in keeping the proper relationship between these two territories as we grow towards natural and supernatural maturity. The ideal situation exists when grace and nature grow side by side, each helping the other to attain that wholeness which God has intended. It is hoped this book will help those who are on their way toward this goal of unity.

Much more could be written about each of the topics treated here. Many assumptions have been made concerning the previous knowledge of the readers. It is presumed that the reader is a Christian who already possesses the wonderful gift of supernatural faith in the Scriptures and in the good news of salvation as preached by Jesus Christ. Throughout this book it is assumed that man is naturally both spiritual and material. The supernatural life of grace is beyond both the natural life of man's soul as well as his body. Grace is the elevation of the whole life of man, both spiritual and physical, to the level of God's life. By sanctity or super-natural maturity we mean this incarnation of human nature into the divine life of grace. To be complete, the Christian saint should also possess a high degree of natural maturity. The attainment of this wholeness requires the cooperation of God, ourselves and our brethren.

No attempt has been made to give a complete descrip-tion of growth in supernatural and natural maturity. As far as grace is concerned, only those topics have been chosen which nearly all Christians share in common—Baptism, Confirmation, Penance, Eucharist. We have discovered anew in our day the value of "togetherness." We now realize that the most important fact in our lives is not whether we are a priest, a sister or a layman; rather it is our Christian faith which we have in common with all other Christians. Our baptismal vows are considerably more important than any other vow we may make later in life.

Side by side with the emphasis on the community, there is a great new emphasis in our day upon the importance of the personal. Other ages of Christianity have insisted upon the value of the community to the neglect of the individual or vice versa—the importance of the individual to the neglect of the group. It is perhaps the genius of our present age to strike the delicate balance that is needed between these two extremes. Both in the field of grace and that of nature there is an ever-present danger of our going to extremes. There is no easy solution to the problem. It is only by living and suffering under this tension that we are able to grow towards that wholeness of nature and grace which we all desire.

Nearly twenty years ago Cardinal Suhard in his great pastoral letter, "Growth or Decline," called for a new Summa of the old and new knowledge applicable to this new age into which the whole world was emerging. Pope John XXIII answered this plea of Cardinal Suhard by calling the Second Vatican Council to give us an *"aggiornamento"*—a bringing up to date of our whole Christian faith. This book is an attempt to carry on the work of synthesis of old and new by giving a brief description of some of the requirements for personal and community sanctity and maturity in this "New Day."

I

A New Day

"In the beginning God created the heavens and the earth; the earth was waste and void; darkness covered the abyss and the Spirit of God was stirring above the waters. God said, 'Let there be light,' and there was light. God saw that the light was good. God separated the light from the darkness, calling the light Day and the darkness Night. And there was evening and morning the first day" (Gn 1:1-5). God began his creation with a new day, filled with light, peace and joy. Then sin entered the world and darkness covered the earth for a long time. With the coming of Abraham, dawn began to appear in the skies. Isaia and the other prophets spoke of a great new day of the Lord that would soon come. "The people who walked in darkness have seen a great light; upon those who dwelt in the land of gloom, a light has shone. You have brought them abundant joy and great rejoicing . . . for a child is born to us, a son is given us . . . His dominion is vast and forever peaceful" (Is 9:1-6).

The Gospels tell us that this prophecy of Isaia was fulfilled with the coming of Christ, the light of the world (Mt 4:16). "In him was life and the life was the light of men. And the light shines in the darkness and the darkness grasped it not" (Jn 1:4-5). For a while the light of this new day shone brightly upon the earth. "I have come a light into the world that whoever believes in me may not remain in darkness" (Jn 12:46). Then evil once again overcame the

14

light. "This is your hour and the power of darkness" (Lk 22:53). However on this occasion the victory of darkness over light was only an apparent one. "Late in the night of the Sabbath, as the first day of the week began to dawn . . . an angel of the Lord came down from heaven. . . . His countenance was like lightning and his raiment like snow. . . . The angel spoke and said to the women, 'Do not be afraid; for I know that you seek Jesus who was crucified. He is not here for he has risen even as he said' " (Mt 28:1-6).

With the resurrection of Christ, another new day had dawned upon the world. Since that time we have been able to walk in the light of the risen Christ. Each day that has been given us during the intervening centuries has been a new day of grace, and though at times evening has come and we have experienced darkness for a short time, we know that never again will the darkness of sin overcome the light of God's grace. Each morning we are able to start afresh with new grace and courage. Each Eucharist we celebrate during the year is a new day of grace, a new union with Christ, our beloved. No matter how many years we live in this present dispensation, there is always something refreshing about each new day. God never repeats himself; each dawn we are able to rise to some surprise our Lord has reserved to give to us at this particular moment. Provided we do our best to cooperate with these new graces, there should never be occasion when we grow tired of God or our religion. If thought of the future does not fill us with enthusiasm and the joy of anticipation, then somehow we are failing to make use of the grace that has been given us. Every day should be a day of growth toward natural and supernatural perfection. There will be many ups and downs along this path to maturity and sanctity, but if we are faithful, the light of grace and love should burn even brighter and brighter.

From time to time during the course of the centuries, there has risen an exceedingly luminous sun of grace. We of this generation are experiencing one of these days. Pope John XXIII prayed for a new Pentecost in our time, a new outpouring of God's Holy Spirit upon the earth. God seems to be answering the good Pope John's prayer and those of many others. We today are experiencing a greater manifestation of God's love perhaps than any other age of Christianity. Both naturally and supernaturally the world is making tremendous advances in knowledge. The extraordinary light of truth that has been given us in our time demands that we correspond with it and work to make our age one of great grace for all mankind. The threat of nuclear warfare gives us added incentive to go all out in leading the world toward good rather than allow ignorance or malice to throw the progress of man backward for a tremendous loss.

Today, none of us can afford to be mediocre. We are all called to be saints according to the particular state of life God has destined for us, and must bear witness to the truth of Christ by the shining light of a life of total dedication to God. A martyr is one who bears witness to truth with his whole life, and when necessary, with his death. In our age the Church has need of great armies of martyrs who are so convinced of the value of the good news of Christ that they will gladly give their lives for his sake. We must all be dedicated apostles in bringing the message of salvation to our brethren. Having received so much light and love from our heavenly Father, we must not be satisfied until we have shared our riches with the whole world. It is the will of God that all men be joined into the one great family of Christ.

Let no one complain that there is nothing to do. Both naturally and supernaturally there are immense tasks awaiting each of us. The great synthesis of the natural and supernatural, so much needed today, will require the combined efforts of many minds and many hands. Divine providence has given our present age the task of striking a balance between nature and grace, individual and community, body and soul, God and man. We have been given the light to see both sides of the truth at the same time. We have now the gigantic task of formulating the many laws that must govern the delicate balance between these extremes. This is especially necessary in the field of natural and supernatural love which is at present so prominent in the thoughts and desires of mankind. Within the past generation we have discovered a whole new world of love, and now, like Christopher Columbus, it is our task to find the best routes to these new lands. Next we must find a way of uniting the old cultures with the new, and so lay the foundations of another age of the world that perhaps will be more glorious than any of the past. What a joy it is for us to work in the early morning dawn, preparing the way for those who will come after us.

All of life is progress towards the last day when Christ will come to establish his kingdom in its fullness. On that, the greatest of all days, everything will sparkle with the brightness of a renewed creation. Truth and love will reign supreme upon this earth. The darkness of error and the coldness of hate will be banished forever from the world. The Lord will separate the wheat from the cockle which, until now, have been allowed to grow side by side. Separated forever from all evil, the good will be able to enjoy an everlasting life of love in the kingdom of God upon earth. "I saw a new heaven and a new earth. For the first heaven and the first earth passed away. And I saw the holy city, the New Jerusalem, coming down out of heaven from God, made ready as a bride adorned for her husband. And I heard a loud voice from the throne saying, 'Behold the dwelling of

God with men. He will dwell with them and they will be his people and God himself will be with them as their God. And God will wipe away every tear from their eyes. And death will be no more, neither shall there be mourning nor crying nor pain any more, for the former things have passed away.' And he who was sitting on the throne said, 'BEHOLD, I MAKE ALL THINGS NEW' " (Ap 21:1-5).

II

Growth in Wholeness

In the rhythm of life we are born, grow, die and are reborn many times. In order to reach wholeness, it is necessary that we die continually to the things of the past so that we can be born again on a higher level of life. Each of these deaths is a crisis in our life by which we are given the freedom to choose a higher and apparently more difficult way of life or to regress to a lower, more mediocre and less demanding way of existence. The decisions we make during these crises will determine the future course of our life, both for nature and for grace. It is especially at these critical moments that we are masters of our own destiny, capable of taking our lives into our hands and of deciding in which direction we will go. Each time we sacrifice something of the past that is near and dear to us, and choose a better way of life, we are paying the necessary price for growth in wholeness.

Sacred Scripture gives a name to this death of the old and resurrection to a new life—in the original Greek it is called *"metanoia."* It may be translated as conversion, penance, or renewal. The verb form is "to repent," "to do penance," "to be converted," "to be renewed." In the Gospels, our Lord and St. John the Baptist both insist on the necessity of metanoia in order to enter the kingdom of God. In the Acts of the Apostles, St. Peter, St. Paul and the other apostles speak of metanoia and faith as the two dispositions

19

necessary for Baptism and the life of grace. Faith is the positive side of conversion—having turned away from the evil or less good, we must make a commitment to something good or better. St. Paul describes the whole process as the death of the "old man" of sin and the resurrection of the "new man" of grace. It is not enough to experience this death and resurrection once at Baptism. It is only by suffering many deaths and enjoying many resurrections that natural and supernatural maturity will be attained. Ideally, the growth in wholeness of nature and grace should progress side by side. In practice, they are seldom together; nevertheless any progress towards perfection of the one will make it easier to endure the necessary metanoia for growth in the other.

It is impossible to bring either our natural or supernatural life to a dead stop, without any movement forward or backward. Whenever we stop growing toward a greater wholeness, somewhere deep in our being we start regressing. In a natural way, these regressions show themselves in psychosomatic illnesses, disturbing dreams, a general lack of peace and confidence in our life, anxieties and neurotic fears. Our hearts dry up, become cold and hard, unable to go out toward others in genuine love. Supernaturally, our prayers become full of distractions, and our whole relationship with God is lacking in enthusiasm and joy. We become pessimistic about the future—the world, the Church, even the providence of God. Our efforts to do good seem more and more useless and sterile, and a sour, bitter attitude infiltrates our whole life.

On the other hand if we are willing to suffer through each crisis and keep going toward something higher, a new and glorious resurrection can be expected. At the point of greatest suffering, all may seem to be lost. We will be called upon to die to certain things of the past and to go forward to something new. At each critical point a decision must be made and it is to be expected that sometimes we will take the wrong road, even after weighing both sides carefully. If a wrong choice is made, we must humbly admit our mistake, withdrawing as gracefully as we can, and then look again for the right road. Never should our past mistakes cause us to retreat into a shell or make us unwilling to take new chances when another decision has to be made. In the pattern of growth toward wholeness there will be many false starts, many trials and failures. The important thing is that we keep trying to go higher and higher progressing always toward natural and supernatural perfection.

In order to attain our goal of sanctity and maturity, it is necessary that we be able to control four fears—fear of God, fear of the world, fear of others, fear of ourselves. These fears must be replaced by a well-ordered and balanced love which will give us the confidence to deal properly with these four areas of our life. Everything in life depends upon love, either natural or supernatural. It is through our power to love that we share most in God's life and God's nature. We were created to love and it is impossible to please God except in loving. "God is love and he who abides in love abides in God and God in him. In this is love perfected within us that we may have confidence in the day of judgment. . . . There is no fear in love; but perfect love casts out fear" (I Jn 4:16-18).

Yet, Sacred Scripture also says that "Fear of the Lord is the beginning of wisdom" (Ps 110:10). As in everything else, there is need of a balance between a healthy respect for God and love for God. Our God is both awesome and attractive and we need to keep always in mind these two sides of his nature. While thinking of his justice and holiness, we must also remember his goodness and love. If one is over-impressed by the fear of an avenging God, this is an indication of a lack of balance in one's religious attitude. The exaggerated fear of God may be due to faulty education or may indicate a weak and cowardly personality. Regardless of the cause, these extreme fears of committing sin and losing God result in a loss of freedom on our part and a powerlessness in making decisions. We become prisoners to our own fears, lacking the courage to launch out into the unknown future. Our growth in wholeness is then curtailed and regression to a lower level of life begins.

An exaggerated fear of the world also prevents our progress towards natural and supernatural wholeness. There are those who mistake Christ's warnings concerning the world. It is true that there are powers at work in the world which are hostile to God and to our own best interests. However this does not mean that the world as such is evil. Anything that God creates is good and it is our task to discover this good and help to develop it into the fullness of its perfection. We should be fascinated with the wonderful things of God's creation but without becoming a slave to them. God created man as lord of the universe and intends that all the creatures of nature should be our servants. We must respect and love these servants, we must try to use them according to the purposes for which God intended them, but never should we allow the world to control us through slavish fear of it.

A third fear that hinders our making the right decisions for growth is fear of our fellow-man. Instead of feeling inferior before others, we need to be conscious of our brotherhood with all the members of the human family. We are all children of the same heavenly Father, and we are all struggling together toward the goal of perfection. In our efforts to reach maturity and sanctity, we need each other. We should be humble and loving enough to ask for help without feeling that we have lost any of our human dignity; at the same time we should be ready to help others in all their needs. Through these situations of need and help we come to realize our mutual creatureliness and our real brotherhood with one another. We must strive to strike a balance between an exaggerated dependence on others and a proud independence of them. When something goes wrong, the primary concern should not be an effort to place the blame on someone; but rather for all of us to work together to remedy the situation as best we can. At one time or another we have all been guilty of wrong-doing; therefore, all of us are partly responsible for the troubles of the world.

A fourth fear to be overcome is an egocentric fear of ourselves and of our ability to succeed. We must have enough self-knowledge and enough confidence in our own worth, to believe that with God's help we can reach the goals of perfection for which we were destined. Trusting ourselves to God and to the powers and talents of our own inner development, we must allow God's providence to mould us according to his own pattern. It may be quite different from what we, or others, have superficially judged to be best for us; nevertheless, we must courageously go forward toward an ever higher goal. To keep progressing toward the wholeness of nature and grace, it will be necessary for us to overcome many fears in regard to ourselves. Frequently the fear most difficult to conquer is the fear of sex. It is often possible to judge one's growth in maturity by the facility with which one handles the precious gift of sex according to the particular state of life to which one has been called. Both married and single people must learn the difficult art of sublimating sex attraction so that when necessary its power can be siphoned off into the higher forms of love and service toward others. For those who lead a celibate life, all of the physical attraction of sex can, and must, be incarnated into spiritual love. When we have attained this ability, we usually lose that exaggerated fear of self which prevents growth in maturity.

To overcome these four fears, it is necessary to endure much suffering. Instead of running away from the difficulties of life, we should be grateful for them. Without problems and crises to be conquered, few would have the courage to attain the high goals God has destined for us. Always our greatest and most constant struggle in life will be to overcome fear and replace it with love—love of God, love of our brethren, a proper love for ourselves and for the world. God has endowed man with an unlimited power to love. By the help of God's grace and with supreme effort on man's part, it is possible to control this power and direct it towards the proper goals. Because of the dangers that result from its abuse as well as its unlimited possibilities for good, it is essential that we know all we can about natural and supernatural love.

III

The Nature of Love

Knowledge—Revelation—Benevolence—Union

There is such an infinite variety to love that every experience of love is different. Nevertheless it is possible to discern four distinct elements in each authentic encounter of love between two persons; whether they be God and myself or another human being and myself. We first become aware of love when we find ourselves desiring to know all we can about that person. This is followed by a desire to reveal ourselves to the beloved. A third desire is the effort to do all we can to please the other, either God or man. Finally, all lovers desire to be united with each other as far as possible. Whenever these four dispositions are present in both parties to the love, we have that perfection of love so desired by everyone.

The first great delight experienced by a lover is the fascination he feels for everything about the beloved. He is tremendously attracted towards the least detail of the other's character and life. Everything he sees strikes a responsive chord within his own being. Having discovered this new world of the beloved which he had never previously suspected to exist, his one great interest in life is to study the object of his love. The more he learns, the more attracted he becomes to the other person. Never was the process of learning so enjoyable as when it is a study of his beloved.

25

Most wonderful of all, the other person seems to possess an inexhaustible store of beauty, truth and goodness.

A lover is not satisfied merely to know all he can about the object of his love. There is a desire to reveal to the other everything about himself. What a joy it is for both to discover how much they have in common—the same secret dreams and desires which they had imagined no one else possessed but themselves. What a delightful surprise it is to find someone with whom one is able to share his most intimate thoughts and hopes. Never again will it be possible to be absolutely alone. There will always be at least one person with whom everything can be shared.

Another desire that manifests itself is benevolence towards the beloved. One wants to do everything possible to make the other person happy. He wants the beloved to be the most perfect, the most beautiful, the happiest person possible, and he will do all in his power to see that this is accomplished. He will go to any extreme to show his love and is willing to dedicate his life to the other, whether that person be God or another human being.

The goal of all true love is a permanent union with the beloved, but this union is possible only if the other person also desires it. Both parties must freely choose to give themselves in love to each other, otherwise no real union can be attained. Nevertheless, the lover will do all in his power to encourage the other to say "yes" to his proposal of love. If his love is great, he will literally beg for a return of love, exposing his whole soul to the possibility of being deeply hurt if his offers are spurned. Union with the beloved becomes for him the pearl of great price that makes no sacrifice too great, no price too high, to attain his goal.

Difficulties in Love

It is easy to see the possibility of great suffering when we open ourselves to love, since one can never be sure what response the other will make to our invitation. Because of the danger that the offer of love will be spurned, many people are afraid to love. However those who have once tasted the wonderful joys of love will usually be willing to pay the high price required of a lover. This is why it is so important to give others, especially the young, as many experiences of unselfish love as it is possible for us to give. If they have had a number of satisfying encounters of being loved and cherished, they will then be more ready to open their own hearts toward others. Love or lack of love experienced in childhood and youth greatly influences the ability to love and be loved in adult life.

Love would be difficult enough if we had to contend only with ourselves, but both parties must freely accept and follow all four of the desires necessary to the fullness of love. In the first glow of attraction, everything may seem easy of attainment, but actually a life-time of effort is required to bring love to a successful completion. This is true not only of marriage but of every worthwhile friendship, including that between God and ourselves. In the present condition of life suffering in some form will always be connected with love. Even our Lord and the Blessed Mother were unable to love without passing through the crucible of pain. The greater the worth of the love, the higher the price that we will need to pay. During the growth of love toward union there usually develops a number of crises of which the outcome is uncertain. Either there will be doubts about our own ability to measure up to the demands of the love, or we must await the decision of the other party to make a return of our love.

Crisis in Knowledge

It is possible for a crisis to develop at any step along the path to love. We may be greatly fascinated at first, but as we come to know the other person more intimately, we may find many things that we do not like. The beloved may also discover qualities in us that are not pleasing. With each of these crises a decision has to be made to continue or terminate the relationship. A mature individual will weigh both sides and make a free decision in the best interests of both parties.

Crisis in Revelation

In the process of opening ourselves to the beloved, other crises may arise. There may be secrets of our past life which we hesitate to reveal. We are torn between the desire to be completely open with the other and the fear that the relationship will end if the beloved knows us as we really are. The more insecure we are, the more fearful we will be of losing the other's love. Those who have a particularly low opinion of themselves and are lacking in self-confidence will go through intense suffering when they expose the secret depths of their souls to the beloved.

Crisis in Benevolence

In the beginning there seems to be nothing that we would refuse to make the beloved happy. Sooner or later, however, there will be clashes between our own selfish interest and service to the other. In the intimacy of love it is not possible to conceal our basic selfishness from the eyes of the beloved. We grow tired or lazy and find the constant effort to please the other person too much trouble. If the beloved is also selfish, it becomes even more difficult for us to keep putting out the effort needed to serve him. We will see how the other takes advantage of our love and often demands an unreasonable service of us. In these conflicts of interest, decisions must be made, and sometimes it will be judged necessary to terminate the relationship. At other times, the value of the love is so great that one makes a decision to increase his generosity and benevolence toward the other instead of compromising it.

Crisis in Union

Many different degrees of union are possible with the beloved. We are capable of real union only with another person, not with an animal or a thing. The more mature both are, the more perfect can be the union; and the more areas of life where both find a true compatibility, the easier it will be to attain unity. This agreement should exist at least on the ultimate questions of life. Both should have more or less the same depth of emotional life as well as the same level of intellectual and cultural values. Because of original sin, our ability to love has been seriously weakened. Ordinarily we are capable of having only a few close friendships in life, and even these need special help from God in order to develop and persevere. The greater one's capacity for love, the higher the price that must be paid to fulfill this potential.

Unless these souls have been very thoroughly trained in self-control and generosity, there is grave danger that they will refuse to make the sacrifices necessary for the union of love. Instead of progressing forward into greater maturity, they may choose to regress in time of crisis. At the moment they imagine that the lower level of existence offers greater attractions than the higher but more difficult unity with the beloved; but as time goes on, they find their lives becoming more and more frustrated. In the dissatisfaction with their present state, God is calling them to reverse their former decision and to return to the tasks of love.

If they obey this call of grace, they can regain their earlier losses, provided they are willing to pay an extra price of suffering and effort. Anyone who has tasted the joy of love will not have to be convinced of the value of friendship. The problem exists for those who for one reason or another have never had a true experience of love. Words have never been capable of adequately describing the beauties of love. The only way to help a person who does not appreciate love is to give him one's own unselfish love. The older a person is and the more one has been hurt in the past by the lack of love, the more difficult it is to penetrate the hard shell that has grown around his heart. Nevertheless, love is so exceedingly good that we should go to any extreme to help others experience this most wonderful of all God's powers that he has shared with man.

If we have been recipients of a true and unselfish love from our parents, teachers and friends, then we have a grave duty to share it with others who have not been so blessed. Our hearts should go out in friendship to every neglected soul and every hardened heart. Their inability to love is nearly always due to an excessive fear of God, themselves, others or the world. They may be afraid of having their love rejected, afraid of being hurt should they expose their hearts to others. They may be lacking in the necessary inner security that is needed to bestow their hearts in love upon others. Perhaps due to a faulty education, they may imagine that they will offend God if they allow themselves to love human beings. Regardless of the cause, they need help and it is our duty to go out to them in love.

IV

The Objects of Our Love

There are many kinds of love, depending upon the particular object which we love. In general, these objects fall under four headings—God, our neighbor, the world and ourselves. Strictly speaking, it is possible only to love another person— whether that person be God, an angel or another human being. Nevertheless, in our ordinary human speech, we speak of loving money, loving ourselves, loving the world. It is possible to use love in this loose sense as long as it is a question of a desire on our part to be united with the object of our love. Our union with an inanimate object is of an entirely different nature from the union of love with another person. As long as we keep this distinction in mind, we can speak of a proper love of ourselves and the world, as well as of God and our neighbor.

The beginning of all love is respect for the object to be loved. Persons and things are to be treated with reverence for their nature and purpose and not merely in accord with our own selfish desires and needs. This reverence is especially necessary in all our relationships with God. The familiarity of our love for God must always bear in mind the infinite distance that separates us from our Creator. Nevertheless fear of God should never dominate our prayers and other actions toward God. God has called us to love him with our whole heart, with our whole soul, with our whole strength and with our whole mind (Lk 10:27). This first and greatest commandment of God should leave no doubt in our minds about the all-importance of love in our relationships with God. It is the greatest of all possible loves that we can experience, either in this life or in the future life. All other loves should be a training ground to prepare us for this supreme love of God.

After God, our greatest love should be bestowed upon other human beings. There are three general forms of human love—parental, brotherly and spousal. Each of these is different, yet all of them contain the four elements explained in the previous chapter. If both parties to the love freely choose to make the necessary effort to develop all four of these desires or dispositions, then they will experience true love, that most wonderful of all God's gifts. To reach maturity, the normal person needs to know something about all three loves—love of parents, love of friends or brethren, love of a person of the opposite sex. At one time or another in our life we need to have been loved by parents or by someone who took the place of parents; by someone whom we can call a friend or brother; by someone we can consider a spouse, either naturally or supernaturally. To attain wholeness in our own life, we need to have given ourselves in love to others; first as a child to a parent and later as a parent to children, whether they be physical children or our spiritual children; secondly, as a friend to our brethren; thirdly, either naturally or supernaturally, as a spouse to another spouse. The more experience we have of love, the more mature we should become. Experiences in natural love should make it easier for us to love God and our brethren supernaturally. There is always a necessary order and balance among the many different persons we are obliged to love. Since our time and energy are both limited, we must make our decisions of love according to the particular needs of all those involved. Mistakes will be often made in our decisions of love, but if we are sincere, God will protect us. The important thing in life is that we do not stop loving others as best we can.

Besides the love we should give to God and our brethren, there are two lesser forms of love that are also necessary —love of the world and love of ourselves. The danger of going to excess in our love for the world and ourselves is considerably greater than when we are loving God and our fellow human beings. For one thing, it is beneath our human dignity to seek the same intimate union with things of the world or with our own ego that we should desire with God and other persons. Union of love implies equality and it is never right to put ourselves on an equal level with an animal, money, property, pleasure, or our ego. It is even worse when we allow these lower creatures to enslave us so that they become our masters and we their servants.

Probably the greatest of all dangers lies in becoming enslaved to our ego. The ego is the center of our conscious life; the real center of our nature is the person or the self, which is hidden in the unconscious. Sacred Scripture commands us to love this inner "self" and gives it as the standard for our love of our neighbor. "Thou shalt love thy neighbor as thy *self*" (Lk 10:28). Problems arise when we substitute the ego as the center of our lives. This easily degenerates into a worship of our ego which we sometimes call self-idolatry or self-worship. In like manner when we speak of selfishness, we really mean egotism.

According to C. G. Jung, the fundamental task in attaining maturity is to establish the authenticity of the ego. This means that it must be trained to know and keep its proper place as the servant of our inner being, which in turn will be subject to God and God's laws. When Adam's inner self rebelled against God, Adam's ego in turn rebelled against his own inner self. Instead of remaining a servant to the self, the ego sought to become the king and master of man's whole nature. Authenticity is established when the ego is brought under control and taught to be a good prince in the service of the real king—our inner self or person. If the ego will work hard to perform its appointed tasks, it will succeed in centering all the powers and faculties of our nature in our person and not in the ego.

One of the tests of a well-centered and authentic person is the absence of anxiety and insecurity in regard to himself. Instead of fear, our attitude should be one of love—a proper, well-ordered love, but, nevertheless, real love for ourselves. Unless we have a proper respect for ourselves, we will never be able to enter into the proper relationship of love with God and our fellow human beings. Authenticity of the ego, therefore, is the foundation for all other growth towards wholeness, both natural and supernatural. It is impossible for the egocentric person to be either a saint or a naturally mature man. The reason is that an egotist does not know how to love or chooses to love the wrong things and in the wrong order.

The tasks of love are without a doubt the most important of all the work given man to accomplish. The success of everything, both natural and supernatural, depends upon the happy solution of the many problems involved in our learning to love. We cannot expect any easy or quick attainment of perfection in this art. It requires a lifetime of struggle amid countless conflicts. The greater our capacity for love, the more difficult it will be to control this. This, however, does not mean that we need to be fighting continuously. There is a time for the enjoyment of the peace and other wonderful fruits of love. The more proficiency we have attained in our ability to love, the greater and more frequent will be our periods of joy and happiness with our friends. Even for those who must work hard to develop their extraordinary potential, there is need for periods of quiet enjoyment of their love. On the other hand, if we find ourselves going through life without any real struggles or conflicts with egocentricity or other abuses, this is nearly always an indication that we have stopped increasing our capacity for love and have settled for a life of mediocrity.

The area of our greatest struggle is usually the conflict between nature and grace. In the original plan of God, there was no problem between man's natural life and his life of grace. On the last day, in the renewed creation, once again nature and grace will live peacefully together. The more mature and holy we become on earth, the less conflict we will experience between these two territories of our life. However, for most of us during the major portion of our earthly life, we will experience great difficulty in keeping a healthy balance. Many people try to solve this constant tension between nature and grace by denying the validity of the one or the other. Those who have chosen a life of nature will refuse to believe in the reality of the supernatural life of grace. Sometimes those who have made a choice of grace, are inclined to consider the things of nature as evil and opposed to grace-life. Any sort of dualism is contrary to the whole revelation of Christ, which insists that nature not be destroyed but be incarnated and lifted up to the level of grace. Grace is supposed to build upon nature, and the more sound and healthy is our whole nature of body and soul, the less difficult it will be to attain supernatural sanctity. As far as possible, growth in natural maturity should keep pace with growth in sanctity. We must struggle to attain this constant balance and tension between the two, but it is a consolation to know that the more we grow in wholeness, the less difficult the effort becomes. What a joy it is to discover that ultimately and basically there is no actual conflict between natural and supernatural love!

V

Natural Love of God

The ultimate goal of all love is the love of God. Other forms of love have value in themselves, nevertheless they would never have existed except through creation by God's love. If we use these created loves properly, they will always lead us toward the love of God and never away from it. Among God's created loves which he has seen fit to share with us, we can distinguish two fundamental categories. In the first category is included all those natural forms of love about which we spoke in the last chapter. The second category is the higher and more important one—the supernatural love which we call grace-life.

One might imagine that a study of nature would yield unquestioning proof of God's love for man. If man had not sinned, this would have been the case. The face of God presented to man in the garden of paradise was clearly that of pure love. However, the adversary of God convinced the first parents that what they saw had only the appearance of love. They were led to believe that God was actually hostile to their best interests, keeping them from becoming like himself. By allowing Satan to deceive him, the first man was responsible for the darkening of the intellect that followed. Since the fall, we often find it hard to see the loving hand of God behind the outward appearances of evil. Man deliberately chose to consider as evil something that was actually only difficult of attainment. Throughout the history of the world, mankind has been guilty many times of the same mistake that is symbolically represented in the first chapters of Genesis. God's will has been considered hostile to man's best interests because God does not give us the reward of love without strenuous efforts on our part. This hostility to God which is present within each of us is called by St. Paul the "sarx." Unfortunately this has been usually translated as the "flesh" (Gal 5:17). We will explore this problem more fully in Chapter Fifteen.

In man's laziness, he would like love to be soft and easy of attainment. Actually love is the fruit of labor and those who are unwilling to work do not receive the joy of love. At first sight, it may seem that the greater good for man would be to have a life of unending ease and comfort. In reality, this is contrary to man's nature as well as God's nature. "My Father works even until now and I work" (Jn 5:17). When man was created and placed in paradise, he was commanded to dress and keep the garden. It is a likely supposition that if Adam and Eve had obeyed God and had been busy at their work, Satan would never have been able to conquer them. Now that we live under the curse of Adam's sin, the effort necessary to attain love is even greater. "Cursed be the ground because of you; in toil shall you eat of it all the days of your life; thorns and thistles shall it bring forth to you. . . . In the sweat of your brow shall you eat bread" (Gn 3:17-19).

When a child is suffering from the chastisement of an angry father, it is quite difficult to realize that the hand that strikes is a loving hand. Nevertheless common sense tells us that this can be true. Therefore when we study nature today, it is possible to see the love of God even in the thorns and thistles that now form our punishment. "The discipline of the Lord disdain not; spurn not his reproof; for whom the Lord loves, he reproves and he chastises the son he favors" (Prv 3:11-12). Granting the fact of sin in the world, we should realize the need of suffering and hard work in order to find the love that is still man's goal. Even in the garden of paradise, it was necessary to struggle in order to overcome temptations against love. How much more difficult it is now.

Contaminated as we are by the blindness of Adam's sin, it is rather easy for us to conjure up the picture of a hostile God, lacking in genuine love for us. Without supernatural grace we would never be able to see through the appearances of evil in nature and discern the loving hand of a heavenly Father behind them. But even with the graces of supernatural faith, great effort on our part is required to see God's love in nature and to make a return of this love to God and our fellow-men. This uncertainty of all natural love serves a very useful purpose in bringing out our real character. Anyone can love when it is easy. True love is proven best in times of crisis. In difficulties we may be tempted to think that God is not interested in us; he appears to be anything but a benevolent God. We search for God and he seems to have withdrawn from us and to be hiding from us. We look for the four elements of love in God's dealings with us and we imagine that none of them can be found. For a time our whole relationship with him hangs in the balance just as it did during the temptation of Adam and Eve in the Garden. Each of us is called upon to make a decision either for or against God.

It is during these critical moments of life that nature needs help from the outside. If the crisis is not too great, another human being may be able to restore our faith and trust in a loving God. Frequently only supernatural grace can redeem us from the depth of despair which we now may feel toward God. But grace alone is not enough; there must be a willingness on our part to accept that grace and cooperate with it. In Sacred Scripture God has promised to be faithful to us and give us the supernatural aid to overcome our natural despair (I Cor 10:13). He promises to enlighten our minds to know and see the truth of God's love (Phil 2:13). We have his assurance that grace will strengthen our wills to make the effort necessary to love. But never will our divine lover force us against our wills to make a decision to love him. If we use our freedom to decide against God, it will not be because we lacked the necessary light and strength from God to accept his love. Like Adam, we may blame Satan and evil companions for influencing us, but ultimately, the responsibility will be our own.

It is a difficult task to have an encounter of love with anyone, and when this person is God, the effort required is exceedingly great. Some people have the idea that loving God is easy. We little realize that if God should appear before us in all his tremendous power, we would be so overawed that we would only want to flee from his sight. God told Moses, "My face you cannot see for no man sees me and still lives" (Ex 33:20). Even the voice of God makes us tremble with fear: "On hearing [the voice] the disciples fell on their faces and were exceedingly afraid" (Mt 17:6). God is quite different from the idea most of us have of him, and without a deep conversion of this knowledge of God, it is impossible to have a true union of love with him. We must allow our nature to be transformed until it is capable of meeting God on a divine level. Natural effort cannot do this. Supernatural help is necessary for this transcendence to take place; and frequently our nature rebels against such an incarnation. We do not want to abandon the habitat of nature because it seems at first sight that the supernatural will destroy the natural. If we imagine that the love of God requires the loss of our nature, we will resist such a change with all the powers of our natural being. We do not want to open ourselves in love to a God who will compel us to abandon all that we have come to cherish in our nature.

Many crises will develop in our attempts to attain even a natural union of love with God. Again and again we may question the value of the four elements necessary for a sincere love of him. We are not so sure that we *do* want to know all about this God who at times seems so cruel and unjust. We hesitate to open ourselves to a God in whom we find it difficult to have complete confidence. We have no feelings of benevolence toward one who appears so often to be anything but benevolent himself. We have no desire for any union of love with a God who seems so contradictory in many of his actions. If left to his own natural efforts, in this present order man would always have a distorted picture of God, who would be impossible to love. In the first article of his *Summa Theologica,* St. Thomas Aquinas puts it very nicely, "The truth concerning God, investigated by natural reason, will be attained by very few men, only after a long time and even then with an admixture of errors" (Pars Prima, Q. 1, A. 1).

The natural history of mankind is living proof of the necessity of supernatural revelation and grace for a true knowledge and love of God. At the same time the depth psychologists have proved in a scientific way that there is a natural capacity in man's nature to know and love God. Just as we have the five senses to make contact with material reality, so God has implanted certain spiritual organs in our souls that are called archetypes. They enable us to make contact with the spiritual world and, if properly developed, they enable us to enter into a natural relationship of love with a supreme being. It is the task of all religions to develop these natural, religious capacities in the hearts of men. If these religious archetypes of man are left undeveloped, all kinds of neurotic conflicts result, especially during the second half of man's life on earth. Therefore, even from the point of view of natural maturity, it is necessary that man establish a proper relationship with God. Not only does the mature man need a love-relationship with himself, with the world and with his human brethren; he cannot attain the wholeness of his nature without a loving relationship with God.

Instinctively or intuitively realizing their need for God, nearly all of mankind has sought this relationship through the practice of some sort of religion. Unfortunately one of the effects of original sin was that man's intellect was darkened and his whole personality weakened. However, God did not abandon man to his ignorance and helplessness. Divine revelation was given to Adam even as he was expelled from the garden of paradise. Supernaturally, God has come to the aid of man throughout the history of the world. These supernatural revelations and graces were never forced upon him, but were merely offered. At times, man accepted God's special help and benefited greatly from it, but more often than not, he rejected the offer of grace and enlightenment, and attempted to set up some form of natural religion. Before the coming of Christ, when divine revelation was limited to a small group of people, these natural, pagan religions elicited the best that might be expected from most of mankind. With the advent of Christ and the world-wide proclamation of the Christian Gospel, these natural religions were no longer sufficient. More often than not they have become the deadly enemies of Christianity.

In our present Western civilization, natural forms of

religion are practiced in a variety of ways. There are, for example, those who make a religion of service to their fellow-men. They consider the hidden God too far away to be taken seriously; whereas the great needs of suffering humanity are more immediate, so they become great humanitarians and social workers. If very wealthy, they become philanthropists, handsomely endowing different foundations for the betterment of mankind. Often they are sincerely motivated by a genuine love for their brethren, but Christ and the Christian faith may be completely absent from their life, and though this may be considered religious, it is a natural, pagan form of religion.

Others may have some knowledge of God and Christ, but be unwilling to make any commitment to a particular form of religion, remaining outside all organized religious bodies in proud isolation and tolerating the existence of churches only for weak creatures who need these props. For themselves, they are content to stand alone in their man-made relationship with the God of their choice. Because they make their own rules and laws, there will seldom be any conflict between what they want and what they think their God wants.

A third form of natural religion today is the worship of psychology. Because of the tremendous discoveries in this field during the present century and because it is always a temptation for man to worship himself as a god, the cult of psychology is a particularly dangerous form of pagan religion. In no way does this justify our ignoring the new insights into man's nature which the psychologists have discovered in recent generations. Because of the danger of our going astray into false forms of religion, it is all the more necessary for Christians to understand psychology and to help those in this field to see its Christian implications.

Otherwise we may well awaken a generation from now to find on our hands an anti-Christian psychology that would be militantly religious in its efforts to destroy all other forms of religions, including the Christian Church.

There is another form of natural religion that is found among those who are members of Christian churches and who consider themselves practicing Christians. These are the individualists who feel no special commitment towards the Christian community but only personally to God. There is, of course, the need of balance between individual and community and it is possible to go to extremes in either direction. However, our greatest problem at present is awakening individual Christians to the needs of the community. Since liturgy is a group experience, there can be no progress in liturgical worship as long as the majority of the congregation insist on worshiping God in their own private, individualistic way. Because of the lack of authentic liturgical experiences in the recent past, most Christians of our day have had only individual encounters with God, coming to know and love God privately, apart from the community. They have developed their own individual form of prayer-life and worship, even when attending Mass with their brethren. The more satisfaction they have found in these personal encounters with Christ, the more they now resent the distractions of joining in a community form of worship. They feel that they cannot pray or make contact with their God when everyone around them is singing or praying aloud. They think of the church as a quiet place, conducive to deep meditation on the things of God. They feel no obligation towards joining with others to attain a communal encounter with God, since this is a religious experience of which they are completely ignorant. It comes as quite a shock to these people to be told that it is contrary to the Christian religion to insist upon the private character of liturgical worship.

It is necessary that all natural love of God be converted into supernatural love. Unless these natural religious experiences are incarnated and elevated to the supernatural level of grace, they soon become enemies of God instead of friends. Once we grant the fact that God has called man to a supernatural union of love with the Blessed Trinity, all natural forms of religion become invalid. They may serve as teachers who prepare mankind for Christ, but they become deadly enemies of Christianity if they insist on being the highest or best ways of loving God. Depth psychology and the various forms of modern, natural religion can do a great service to Christianity by helping mankind to discover and develop his natural capacity for God. There is a vast portion of the human race in which the natural religious archetypes are still asleep—untamed, uncultivated, untapped. As long as this remains true, these men cannot even attain natural maturity, let alone the supernatural encounters of sanctity. However, there is a danger that in awakening these archetypes of religion, they will be used merely as means towards the development of natural maturity and not primarily for the supernatural encounter with God by grace.

Once our natural capacity for God is awakened, many conflicts will arise between God's interests and what seems to be self-interest. In order to convert our natural love for God into a supernatural love, help from God is needed as well as many sacrifices of our own selfish desires. Any basic change in our nature requires great effort and struggle on our part. But once converted, a wonderful change takes place in our whole being. This awakening of supernatural faith and love for God is immensely greater than the experience of falling in love with another human. Every faculty of our being is aroused and intensified. For the first time, we become aware of our true significance before God. All of our other powers for love are increased so that immense progress is made in the wholeness of nature as well as grace. We now have a true presentiment of what life is really meant to be. Our personality awakens in all its fullness. Through the quiet voice of our conscience, our divine lover reveals to us most intimate secrets and desires. Each time we open our hearts in love and correspond with God's call of grace, our whole being takes another step forward toward natural and supernatural wholeness.

VI

The Grace-Life of Supernatural Love

There are many points of similarity between natural and supernatural love. It will help us to take the four elements of natural love and see how beautifully they apply to God's love for us through sanctifying grace. Strange as it may seem, God is fascinated by us and deeply concerned about each of us. He wants to reveal his whole nature to us and desires to do everything possible to make us happy. Most of all he wills to be united with us forever through this supernatural life which we call sanctifying grace. Grace-life is a supernatural gift from God by which we share the same intimate life and nature as do the Father, Son and Holy Spirit. For God, life and love are interchangeable—to share in God's life means to be loved by him with all the fullness of his being. "I have come that you may have life and have it more abundantly" (Jn 10:10).

In order to become partakers of the divine nature (II Pt 1:4) it is necessary that we freely choose to make a return of love to God in the same measure with which he has first loved us. We must allow ourselves to become involved in a tremendous fascination and attraction for God. Not only must we desire to know all we possibly can about him, we must also try to open ourselves completely to him so that we keep no secrets hidden. Third, our love of benevolence toward God will express itself by a constant desire to please him—to do his will and obey his commands. Finally, we should want more than anything else in the whole world to be united forever in love with our heavenly Father, with Jesus Christ, and with the Holy Spirit.

It should be quite evident that our weakened human nature could never alone accomplish the gigantic tasks expected of us when we love God with a supernatural love. We need special help from God and this comes to us in the form of actual or helping grace. God not only loves us in an infinite, supernatural way, he gives us the power to love him as he loves us. If we fail to make a proper response of love to God's call of grace, we will be able to blame only ourselves. Since no love, natural or supernatural, can ever be forced, God will never compel us, against our will, to make a return of love. The grace-life of God's love is made available to us, and he lets us know in many ways how much he desires to share this life with us. He gives all the helping graces we need to make a return of love on a supernatural level. He then waits for our response.

From the very beginning, God called man to this life of supernatural love. In a symbolic way Sacred Scripture speaks of God walking in the garden with Adam in the cool of the evening (Gn 3:8). This exemplifies the great intimacy that God wishes to have with his beloved creation. Unfortunately man decided to reject God's offer of love and to try to find satisfaction apart from him. However, God's love for man was so great that he continued to invite mankind to this life of grace. Down through the ages there were some who generously responded to God's call to the supernatural life — Noah, Abraham, Moses, Samuel, David, Elias, Isaia, Daniel, John the Baptist. There was one creature who better than any other answered God's loving call of grace—this was the Blessed Virgin Mary at the Annunciation. It was God's choice that through the child born of this woman, the whole of mankind would be given another opportunity to be united in supernatural love with the Blessed Trinity. It is through the Incarnation of Jesus Christ that we today are able to participate in the divine life of grace. Just as the power of God's Spirit lifted up the flesh of Mary and united it to God, so this same Holy Spirit through grace-life, lifts up our body and soul into a supernatural union with God. We may call this our "incarnation."

The law of incarnation will continue its work of uniting God and man through love until the whole of mankind has attained that union with the divinity for which it has been destined. By joining ourselves to Jesus Christ through sanctifying grace, we fulfill this desire for unity with God. Sacred Scripture makes clear to what extremes God is willing to go to attain this love-union with man. On the other hand, the history of mankind gives abundant illustration of the desire of man to partake of divinity. When this ambition is misdirected it becomes the sin of pride. If we have wisdom, we will know that it is only in submitting ourselves to God's plans that we are able to fulfill these basic desires of ours to be like God. What we cannot do alone through nature, is accomplished in a supernatural way through grace.

Through sanctifying grace, we experience an incarnation that enables us to participate in the same three relationships of love that exist between the Persons of the Blessed Trinity. God the Father becomes our heavenly Father and we his adopted children in the family of God. God the Son becomes our divine Brother and we are united to him in the most intimate bonds of friendship. God, the Holy Spirit, is now our divine Partner through a spiritual union that is considerably more real and meaningful than any union on earth. By means of grace-life the inner depths of our being are touched by the three Divine Persons and our whole nature is transformed. When we are living in grace it is as though a dead electric wire was connected to a giant dynamo, and our whole being is filled with the infinite power and beauty of God's life. As far as God is concerned, he desires that this union with us be permanent. He has promised to give us all the helping graces we need to keep us growing in each of the three loving relationships with the Divine Persons. If we cooperate with grace, we will experience a new incarnation each time a new contact with God is made, so that there is no limit to the heights of love that are available to us. It depends upon our decision when confronted with Christ.

Crisis in Knowledge of God

The interchange of supernatural love between God and man will be filled with crises and struggles similar to those found in natural relationships of love. Because God is so infinite and different from creatures, it is difficult for us to know God as he really is. Indeed, even the words of our languages break down when we try to describe God's nature. Because God wants so much to reveal himself to us, divine ingenuity has devised many ways to allow us to know him. The best of these ways is the Incarnation of the God-man. In Jesus Christ we are able to study God in human form. "He who sees me, sees also the Father" (Jn 14:9). We must allow ourselves to become intrigued with the divine personality of Jesus. If we make the effort to study the life of Christ, we can become so attracted to him that we will want to know everything about him. In the process of getting to know

Christ, we will encounter a number of facets to his personality that will be difficult to accept in all their literal fullness, for example, Christ's insistence on poverty and the danger of riches. Because they conflict with our own selfish desires, we will be tempted to reject them or at least water down their impact. The decisions that we make during these struggles with Christ and our conscience will determine the future course of our relationships of love with Christ and God.

Crisis in Revelation of Ourselves

Other crises develop during the growth of grace-life when we try to be completely open and honest with God. It is often anything but pleasant to admit before him our deep egocentricity and other faults. We are tempted to make excuses for our behavior—trying to blame others, even God, for the way we have acted. We are ashamed to expose our deliberate betrayals of love in the past. If this is the price for growth in supernatural love, we may choose not to pay it. If so, our relationship with God becomes strained. There is danger that we may choose to reject God's love rather than endure the agony of facing before him the full truth about ourselves.

Crisis in Benevolence toward God

A third area of crisis in the progress of supernatural love is the question of how far we are willing to go in order to please God. If we are to love God as he loves us, it is necessary that we make an all-out commitment in our efforts to do his will. Again and again there will arise a conflict between what God wants and what we want. In each of these situations we must make a decision as to whether we will

love God more than we love ourselves. The growth or decay
of our grace-life is determined by our generosity or lack of
generosity in doing God's will. God's helping grace will
always be available, but ultimately, our own free choice will
be the deciding factor in this whole relationship of supernatural love.

Crisis in Union with God

Every form of love has as its goal to be united with the
beloved. In no relationship of natural love is this need of
union as great as it is in the supernatural relationship of
grace. God created the human race in the beginning in order
to unite us to himself in the closest possible bonds of love.
Adam broke these bonds of union, but God's desire for
union is so great that he has persistently created new opportunities for man to be united again in love with his Creator.
Man, for his part, has been almost as persistent in rejecting
the divine offers of love. Much of the history of mankind is
a tug-of-war between man's waywardness and God's loving
kindness in recalling man to the tasks of love. With the
Incarnation, God won the most decisive of all battles in this
struggle. In Jesus Christ, we have an everlasting marriage of
the divine and human natures. In the God-man, we have the
first piece of that united kingdom of heaven and earth which
from all eternity God has desired. Never again will it be
possible to separate God from man, since the Incarnation,
once started, will never end. What took place in the womb
of Mary at the Annunciation, continues to happen each
time we open our souls to the reception of grace. This
grace-life encounters much resistance from those whom it
seeks to incarnate to the divine level of supernatural love.
But we have God's assurance in Sacred Scripture that the

forward progress of the work of Incarnation will never cease. By our refusal to make a return of love to God, we hinder and delay the final day of victory. However, never again will it be possible for mankind to destroy God's plan of a permanent union of love between us. One day, the Last Day, the work of Incarnation will come to an end, because on that day, the greatest of all days, God and all his beloved people will be united forever.

VII

The Third Aeon–Goal of Supernatural Love

All love looks forward with eager longing to a permanent union with the beloved. God's supernatural love desires not only that blessed union with our souls in heaven which we call the beatific vision; he desires to be united with our whole nature, body as well as soul. This will be accomplished only on the Last Day when our bodies will be restored to life and share in the same union of love as the souls of the blessed now enjoy. To emphasize the distinctive character of this new life which we will receive at the Second Coming of Christ, we call it the *Third Aeon*. The first aeon extended from the creation of Adam in paradise until his fall into sin. The second aeon began with the expulsion of Adam from paradise and will continue until the final coming of Christ at the end of time. The third aeon will begin with the renewed creation of the Last Day and will continue here on earth forever. It will be the fulfillment of the Kingdom of God upon earth which began with the Incarnation and is present today in the Christian Church.

In the glorified life of the Last Day, God's love will reach its ultimate perfection and the last and greatest of the "New Days" will dawn upon the earth. The world as we now know it will be transformed and not destroyed. A new heaven and a new earth will rise from the old to become the home of all those who have chosen to make a return of love to God's repeated calls of grace. Only those who will have learned to love, both naturally and supernaturally, will find a place in this third aeon. The time of testing will be over; for all eternity we will be able to enjoy the fruits of the efforts of the second aeon. Never again will we have to struggle and no longer will the outcome of our actions be in doubt. Our final decision for God and for love will have been made; an eternity of peace and happiness will stretch before us.

In the third aeon we will celebrate the glorious marriage of God and man which was the purpose of every one of God's acts of benevolence towards mankind. It will be here in this kingdom of the Last Day that we will see in all its glory what God has had in mind for us from all eternity. At last we will understand what love is and what it can do, when it is God who does the loving. Without any fears of going to excess or any danger of abuse, we will be able to exercise all our desires of love to the heart's content. At every step of the way in the second aeon of our present life we are faced with new crises and conflicts. This phase of proving our love will end with the Second Coming of Christ. No more will we prefer man to God, ourselves to others. The perfect order of loving will have been permanently established, never again to be broken. Without any possible chance of going to extremes, we will be able to give free rein to every desire of love. Not only will we be given the grace to love each Person of the Blessed Trinity with an unlimited love; we will be able to exercise to the fullest all our powers of love toward each of our friends whom we have loved while upon earth. Now in our present aeon, we have to be so careful with our love, lest we abuse it by going to excess or misdirecting it towards a creature to the exclusion of God. With the Second Coming of Christ, all these dangers will disappear, and we will be able to occupy ourselves entirely with loving all persons, both divine and created. "Behold I make all things new. . . . To him who thirsts I will give of the fountain of the water of life freely. . . . I will be his God and he shall be my son" (Ap 21:5-7).

With the final coming of Christ, evil will be banished forever from the face of the earth. No longer will it be possible to be tempted or to sin. Satan and all his powerful forces will have been decisively conquered and exiled forever from the New Jerusalem of the Last Day. Besides moral and spiritual evil, all physical pain and suffering will likewise be removed from this earth. The darkness of error and ignorance will never again be allowed to overshadow mankind. The bright sun of truth will shed its light for all to see. By the light of this New Day we shall know all truth, all wisdom, all love. We shall know God as he knows us. No longer will there be any secrets among the beloved who have joined themselves irrevocably to Christ. We shall know everything we want to know about our friends and we shall be able at last to reveal our whole being to those we love. "And the city has no need of the sun or the moon to shine upon it. For the glory of God lights it up and the Lamb is the lamp thereof. And the nations shall walk by the light thereof; and the kings of the earth shall bring their glory and honor into it. And its gates shall not be shut by day, for there shall be no night there. . . . And there shall not enter into it anything defiled" (Ap 21:23-27).

Here upon earth, in our present vale of tears, every love and joy is clouded by the fact of death. No matter how happy we are, we know that the joy will soon end to be replaced by new crosses, trials and afflictions. Worst of all, the presence of death is a fact we are never allowed to forget. Of all the punishments for sin, death is without a doubt the worst, whether we think of the first death in the grave or the second death of an everlasting hell. No matter how full is our love and happiness in this present second aeon, the fact of physical death always faces us and the danger of second death of mortal sin and hell is ever-present. In the third aeon, the possibility of both these deaths shall disappear. The skies above the New Jerusalem will always be bright, without a single storm cloud to mar a perfect day. "And God will wipe away every tear from their eyes. And death shall be no more; neither shall there be mourning nor crying nor pain any more. For the former things have passed away" (Ap 21:4).

In our present way of life it is possible for us to enjoy three different relationships of love—love of parents, friends and spouse. These human relationships were given to us to prepare us for three similar forms of love with the three Persons of the Blessed Trinity. By means of grace-life we are able here and now to experience the love of a heavenly Father, a divine Brother, Jesus Christ and a spiritual spouse, the Holy Spirit. To the extent that we can enjoy these three relationships of supernatural love, the Kingdom of God has already come for us. Nevertheless, it is a blind and uncertain union of love. We accept it upon faith and are grateful for the possession of it, even though we are aware of how easily we can lose it. All of this will be changed with the Second Coming of Christ when the veil of faith will be removed forever. We will then be able to enjoy in all their fullness these three supernatural relationships of love which we have received through sanctifying grace. God will reveal his fatherhood to us in all its glory; Jesus Christ will show himself to us both as a friend and a spouse; the Holy Spirit will be seen as the bond of love that unites us to God and to each other forever. " 'Come, I will show thee the bride, the spouse of the Lamb.' And he took me up in spirit to a mountain, great and high, and showed me the holy city Jerusalem, coming down out of heaven from God, having the glory of God. Its light was like a precious stone, as it were a jasper-stone, clear as crystal" (Ap 21:10-11).

The glorious Kingdom of God upon earth began with the Incarnation of Jesus Christ in the womb of Mary. Beginning with this first marriage of God and man, the work of incarnation has spread throughout the world by means of grace. The family of God's holy people, which we call the Church, is the Kingdom of God in this second aeon. The resurrected body of Christ was the first piece of the completed Kingdom of the third aeon. By studying the eleven appearances of this glorified Body of our Brother Christ, we can learn much about the state of our own glorified bodies on the Last Day. The glorified Christ is now hidden in the clouds of heaven, seated at the right hand of the Father. At the end of time the clouds will open and we shall see the Body of Christ coming to raise our bodies from the grave and to unite us, body and soul, to God the Father, Son and Holy Spirit. Then will take place, here on earth in the renewed creation, that eternal wedding banquet about which our Lord speaks so often in the Gospels. "Let us be glad and rejoice, and give glory to him; for the marriage of the Lamb has come and his spouse has prepared herself. . . . Blessed are they who are called to the marriage supper of the Lamb" (Ap 19:7-9).

The doctrine of the future life in God's kingdom is one of the most important revelations in the whole Sacred Scripture. We should meditate often upon the countless passages of the Old and New Testament that speak of this third aeon.

If interpreted according to this future dimension, everything in the words and actions of Christ tell us something about the fullness of the kingdom that will be established on the Last Day. Like the early Christians, we should become so fascinated by the third aeon that we will look forward to it with eager longing. Christianity is primarily a religion of the future, not of the past; it is a religion of triumph and joy, not primarily of suffering and death. The glorified body of Christ should dominate our thoughts much more than the passion and death of Good Friday. During this second aeon it is necessary that we keep a balance between the cross and the resurrection, but we must never forget that suffering and death are only temporary means to an everlasting end—the glorious, eternal goal of the third aeon. If we allow ourselves to become truly enthused over this wonderful New Day that awaits us and the whole world, we will be willing to pay the necessary price to grow constantly in grace-life now.

VIII

The Sacraments as Sources of Grace-Life

From all eternity God has desired to share his life of love with us. His first attempt to do this was rebuffed by man. During the long period between Adam and Christ the heavenly Father again and again made efforts to lift up mankind to a supernatural life. Noah, Abraham and Moses responded to God's call of love. Each time this happened, God entered into a covenant of love with them and their descendants. These testaments of friendship required certain promises of love on the part of both God and man. God promised to make them his own people in a very special way. They promised a return of love by being faithful children of God. As long as man was loyal to his promises, the covenant persevered and grew. Unfortunately the descendants of Noah and Abraham broke the Old Covenant by giving their service many times to false gods.

Some two thousand years ago, the heavenly Father chose to make a new and permanent covenant of love. This New Testament would be everlasting because it was made between the heavenly Father and Jesus Christ, the God-man. With the coming of Christ, the final age of the world began. The Kingdom of God upon earth was not established forever, and mankind had a most worthy representative who could make an adequate return of love to the Father. It was the Father's desire that all men should join themselves to Christ by grace and through Christ make their return of love to God. Each outpouring of sanctifying grace resulted in a new incarnation whereby our human nature was lifted up and united to God. This was accomplished in the same way that the first Incarnation took place—by a touching of God's Person to our person. "The Holy Spirit shall come upon thee and the power of the Most High shall overshadow thee; therefore the Holy One to be born shall be called the Son of God" (Lk 1:35).

During his earthly life, Jesus ordinarily bestowed his graces through contact with his physical body. Frequently our Lord would touch the person; at other times he would use the power of his Word to lift up a human being to super-natural union with God. These priestly actions of Christ resulted in the sanctification of the whole person through bestowal of grace-life. The touch of Christ brought health and life to both body and soul. It was a continuation of the work of Incarnation whereby many other persons were lifted up and made members of God's family along with Christ, the first-born. Through contact with Christ, they were able to participate in that wonderful exchange of love that flows between the Father and the Son. Salvation had come to them through union with Christ.

Before Christ ascended into heaven, he gave to the Church the power to carry on this same work of salvation. "As the Father has sent me, I also send you" (Jn 20:21). "He that hears you, hears me" (Lk 20:16). Just as an earthly spouse might be given the "power of attorney" by her husband before leaving on a long journey, so the Church received from Jesus the power to perform the same priestly actions as Christ when he was visibly on earth. It is through contact with the Church that we encounter Christ today. Whenever we are touched by Christ living in his Church, we experience a new incarnation; our whole being is lifted up by grace and united in bonds of supernatural love to God. "Whose sins you shall forgive, they are forgiven them" (Jn 20:23).

The priestly actions of the Church are called Sacraments. Through them the work of incarnation will continue until Christ again returns visibly to earth on the Last Day. The Sacraments retain their effectiveness only during this present "between-time"—between the Ascension and the final coming of Christ. In this present age of the world Christ touches and sanctifies us through the outward signs of the sacraments. Each sacramental touch of Christ's Church today possesses the same unlimited power to elevate us to the divine level of grace as did the actions of Jesus Christ during his public life. The effect of each worthy reception of a sacrament extends far beyond our own individual soul. The entire family of God's holy people also benefits from each new infusion of grace into our person. Our whole being, body and soul, is healed of the wounds of sin and prepared for the day when Christ will establish his Kingdom in all its fullness. The graces of the sacraments gradually release us from the dreadful slavery we now experience in the areas of pain, ignorance, concupiscence and death.

In this book the discussion is limited to the four sacraments that all Christians should have in common—Baptism, Confirmation, Penance and Eucharist. If we will make proper use of these sacraments, we will be able to grow constantly in the life of grace, preparing ourselves for the perfect union of love with God which Christ wants to share with us. Each of these sacraments fulfills a special need in our lives, providing us not only with sanctifying grace but also becoming a ready source of actual graces needed for our growth and perseverance. Two of them, Baptism and Confirmation, are permanent sacraments in the sense that once received, their power to bestow grace is always ready to go to work during the rest of our life on earth, provided we fulfill the proper dispositions. All of the sacraments give grace in proportion to the dispositions of faith, hope and charity which we bring to them. Each sacrament is filled with the infinite power of God and there is no limit to the degree of union with God which we are capable of attaining, provided we cooperate by opening our whole being in generous unselfish love.

The Sacrament of Baptism

Through Baptism our whole nature is consecrated in a permanent way. The character of Baptism works a radical transformation of our whole being and unites us to Christ in such a way that we are made members of his Body and share in all the mysteries of his life—birth, death, resurrection and ascension. This sacrament acts like a giant press which squeezes our whole nature into the mold of Christ. In an instant we are permanently transformed to the very depths of our being into the likeness of Christ. Just as the flesh in Mary's womb was touched by the Holy Spirit and irrevocably transformed into the God-man, so Baptism makes over our whole human nature into new sons and daughters of God, other Christs.

Once received, the graces of Baptism are available to us any moment of the day or night. As long as we remain on earth, we need only to turn on the switch of faith and the giant motors of grace-life, bestowed at Baptism, start humming within the depths of our soul. The more generous and sincere is the commitment of our faith, the more intensely we will be united with God through the grace-life that flows from this sacrament. Frequently the graces of Baptism lie dormant in our souls, like seeds in the cold, winter soil. Regardless of how long they have lain fallow in our hearts, we need only to apply the proper moisture of the tears of conversion, the necessary light of God's truth and the warmth of a generous love for God; immediately the seeds of grace that were first sown at Baptism will spring up into a luscious new growth of supernatural life.

The Sacrament of Confirmation

By Baptism we are born into the family of God; through Confirmation we reach a certain supernatural maturity. Our Confirmation in many ways resembles the turning point in the life of Christ which took place at his Baptism in the River Jordan. This was the end of his hidden life and the beginning of the public life of service to the community of God's people. At his Baptism, the heavenly Father gave Christ the commission to go out and redeem the world. The Holy Spirit came down upon Christ to strengthen him for the tremendous mission assigned by the Father. The same things happen to us when we receive Confirmation. No longer are we allowed to lead the hidden life of a private citizen in the family of God. The bishop, as the representative of the heavenly Father, commissions us to go out and be a good soldier of Christ fighting to establish the kingdom of God throughout the world. The Holy Spirit touches our person and consecrates us to the apostolate of bringing souls into the fold of Christ and helping those who are already there to become more perfect. The very word "Confirmation" means that this sacrament strengthens us for the particular mission assigned to us in the Kingdom of God.

Through the character of Confirmation we are once again pressed into the mold of Christ and given a permanent share in his priesthood. The graces of this sacrament are always available to us, provided we use the right key to release them. The key that unlocks the graces of Confirmation is a generous charity towards Christ and our brethren. As often as we are willing to devote all the energies of our being to the work of the apostolate, immense graces are at once released through the permanent presence of the character of Confirmation within our souls. As Christians, we have been commissioned by Christ to assist him in the priestly tasks of teaching, guiding and sanctifying other souls. If we cooperate with the powers of Confirmation, every possible grace we need will be given us.

The Sacrament of Penance

A third sacrament which is available to all Christians is that of Penance. It is Christ's Easter gift, bestowed upon us as a sacrament of peace, joy and mercy. Penance is a real touching of Christ's healing hand to our wounded souls and bodies. Just as Christ healed the sinners and the suffering of Galilee, so our wounded natures are healed through the Sacrament of Penance. In no sacrament does so much depend upon our preparation for its reception as does Penance. This sacrament has been called "laborious Baptism" because, unlike Baptism, much effort is required on our part to have our sins taken away by Penance. Routine, mechanical confession, without any real conversion of the heart, is not only a waste of time, it is a real insult to the merciful love of our Savior. Before we go to confession we must make the effort to turn away from all attachment to sin and turn back to God with our whole heart and soul. We call this conversion "metanoia" or "spirit of penance." As was explained in the chapter on "Growth in Wholeness," we need to experience many conversions in our progress towards maturity and sanctity. Each reception of the Sacrament of Penance provides us with the wonderful opportunity to reject sin and all false love and dedicate all our energies to a proper love of God and others. This sacramental metanoia requires a real humiliation on our part and often is quite difficult. We must acknowledge God's authority over us and his right to punish us as he sees fit. We must accept our need of begging for mercy from God, realizing that in strict justice we have no right to forgiveness. Relying on God's infinite goodness and promises, we hope to obtain pardon and we humbly ask for it, promising that we will go to any extreme to avoid sin in the future. All of this is necessary in order to possess the proper spirit of penance for a fruitful reception of this sacrament.

We can never be grateful enough for this wonderful sacrament. Without its encouragement, most of us would postpone or neglect entirely the effort necessary to have a proper metanoia. The most difficult part in the whole work of natural and supernatural perfection is the effort required to endure successfully the many conversions of heart needed by us. If we will take seriously our preparation for Penance and not be content with a routine examination of conscience and a mechanical confession, then each reception of this sacrament will be a giant step toward maturity and sanctity. As far as possible, we should make each preparation for the Sacrament of Penance a turning point in our lives. We should try to face boldly the unpleasant truth of one or more of our evil tendencies. If we are honest with ourselves, we will discover many imperfect and shameful attitudes lurking in the depths of our soul. We regress from maturity and sanctity if we ignore them. Whether we recognize these way-ward tendencies in ourselves or not, damage is done unless we honestly do all in our power to transform them into virtues. The graces of the Sacrament of Penance enable us to do just this—to convert our evil into good.

The Sacrament of the Eucharist

There is a fourth sacrament that all Christians should have in common—the Eucharist. Above all else, it is the great bond of unity between God and man and between one Christian and another during this period of the second aeon. We can never say enough about the Eucharist, so we will return to its consideration again and again in the future chapters. It is the sacrament that we receive more often than all the others combined. It completes the work of grace that was begun in the Sacrament of Baptism and continued through Confirmation and Penance. Ordinarily it should be the last sacrament we receive before dying, under the form of Holy Viaticum—food for the journey from this life of grace to life with God in the kingdom of heaven. We call it the "blessed" sacrament because it is the glorified body of Christ and, therefore, the most precious and most holy of all sacraments.

It is important that we make the Eucharist centered in the Father rather than in the Son. The sacramental Christ of the Eucharist is the Father's gift to us to help us go to the Father. It is given us to nourish the grace-life received at Baptism. Through the Eucharist, our love for the Father should grow with each reception. It is a continual expression of the love of the Father for us and our love for him. During holy Mass we should make use of the Eucharist to express the gift of ourselves through Christ to the Father. We should receive it in Communion as the Father's gift, expressing his acceptance of our gifts, his good pleasure with us and his great love for us. The Eucharistic Banquet is a love-feast, an "agape" where all of God's friends should experience a loving encounter with each other as well as with the Father, Son and Holy Spirit. The Sacrament of the Eucharist was never meant to be a mere private union with God to the exclusion of our brethren. Never should we be so conscious of the family of God as when united with Christ in the Eucharist. Instead of considering those around us a distraction, we should desire after receiving the Eucharist to join them in joyous songs of praise and thanksgiving.

Each Eucharist, along with Baptism, Confirmation and Penance, adds to our capacity to know, love and serve God and our brethren. However, the tremendous powers contained in these sacraments will not operate unless we open our hearts in loving response to God's calls of grace. The sacraments unfold their effectiveness in proportion to the dispositions of the recipient. The main dispositions required of us are faith, hope and charity. The more generously we respond to each sacrament by believing, hoping and loving, the more progress will be made towards wholeness and perfection of our being, both naturally and supernaturally. These virtues are actually three steps of supernatural love which we are able to make in reply to God's supernatural invitation to love. Unaided nature would find it impossible to make a single act of faith, hope or charity. On the other hand, grace without the aid of nature is also helpless in eliciting these virtues in us. Only a marriage of God's grace and our cooperation enables us to form the dispositions needed to receive the sacraments profitably.

IX

Man's Response of Faith to God's Call

The first and most necessary disposition for a fruitful reception of the sacraments is faith. Faith is a new incarnation—a new union of God and man upon earth. As the first Incarnation was possible only when Mary freely consented to God's proposal, so faith is born only when we freely choose to respond generously to God's call of love. Every act of faith is the result of the free choice of both God and man; one without the other is never able to give us faith. God's part in faith comes through his helping grace, showered upon every person who comes into this world. St. Timothy assures us that God "wishes all men to be saved and to come to the knowledge of the truth" (I Tim 2:4). These helping graces precede the reception of the sacraments and are even given to souls in the state of mortal sin. They are like sparks of divine fire which God mercifully showers upon all mankind. If we will cherish these sparks and gently fan them with our efforts to love, they will grow into a blazing fire of supernatural faith. Each reception of a sacrament greatly increases both the sparks and our capacity for holding this fire. The Holy Spirit pours out the fires of grace upon every soul willing to receive them. The more generously we respond to grace, the brighter and more intense will faith and love burn in our souls. The more filled we are with the light and heat of faith and love, the more we will warm all our brethren who surround us. The nearer they come to us, the more they will be enlightened by our faith and love. God's helping grace comes to us not only directly but also indirectly through the community of our brethren. Anyone on fire with faith, hope and charity is like a highly charged transformer, throwing off sparks of grace, and we need only draw near, to be influenced by our contact.

Faith in its fullness is primarily an experience of love which can never be explained through words. We need actually to taste it ourselves before we are able to know what people mean when they talk about faith. Faith adds a new dimension to reality; by it we step into a whole new world, the supernatural world of God. Faith is like a breach in the wall that now separates us from God's world. It is the gate that opens into heaven and connects us with the things of eternity. On the Last Day, we will see God face to face, but now during the second aeon we must simply accept all these wonderful things of God on faith. We are like blind men who are forced to "see" through feeling. If we open our hearts generously to the graces of faith, we will begin to experience the realities of God so vividly that it will be almost like seeing them.

Faith begins as a little mustard seed, a tender little plant or a new-born babe. It must be carefully nurtured, especially at first. We must protect it from the cold winds of doubt, from the flames of passion, from the contamination of worldly, faithless companions. We must water it with the tears of our contrition and warm it with the heat of a generous love. It needs the bright sunlight of God's truth as found in Sacred Scripture and the teachings of the Church. Its growth will be aided greatly by the presence of other persons who are filled with strong faith, high hopes and generous love. It grows best in the bosom of the family of God's holy people and during the beautiful experience of a fine liturgical service. Any increase in our knowledge of Jesus Christ will foster a proportionate increase in our faith.

Supernatural faith grows in proportion to our growth in natural maturity. Since faith is a mature encounter of love with God's person, the more mature our own person is, the easier it should be to respond to his call of grace. As we grow in maturity, we grow in the freedom and ability to make decisions for ourselves. Since faith is making a decision for Christ and for God's plans in our regard, natural wholeness enables us to make a better commitment to God. It takes great courage to close our eyes, put our hand into the hand of God and say, "Yes, heavenly Father, I accept your will for me. Lead on. Take me wherever you wish— even to Calvary and death upon a cross." The courage needed for the commitment of faith is both supernatural and natural. God's helping grace will provide the supernatural fortitude, and the more naturally mature and responsible we are, the easier it will be to cooperate with this grace. On the other hand, the more faith we have, the more quickly our nature will grow toward wholeness and perfection.

The challenge of faith should be in proportion to the degree of maturity and responsibility a person possesses. To demand too heroic a commitment from an immature person will do more harm than good. As one progresses through childhood and youth, a more and more generous response of faith should be asked. If the Eucharistic liturgy is celebrated properly for the various feasts of the year, ample opportunity will be given for the community of God's people to make their proper commitment to God. The climax each year will be the renewal of the baptismal vows during the Easter Vigil Service. If the necessary effort is made during Lent to have a good metanoia, everyone in the congregation will be ready to increase his faith on Holy Saturday night according to the particular stage of his natural maturity. Very special and abundant helping grace from God will be available to all taking part in the service. The presence of mature and heroically generous souls among the community will help the less courageous and less generous to rise to the occasion. The whole service should bring a beautiful community and personal experience of faith to everyone who is present.

From a natural point of view, every experience of love with other human beings will be a tremendous boost to our powers of supernatural faith. The more personal is the atmosphere of the home, the parish, the community the easier it will be for everyone present to make the commitment of faith that God expects of him. Natural love should not be considered an enemy to faith, but rather one of its most important allies. Without good experiences of human love, it will be extremely difficult for anyone to make the heroic acts of faith needed for supernatural sanctity. The more selfless and supernatural is this love we receive and give to our brethren, the greater our ability to make the blind commitment to God which we call faith.

Supernatural faith is the divine incarnation of natural faith and trust in God. Natural faith and trust in another human being follow love rather than precede it. There comes a moment in the life of two lovers when one makes a proposal of permanent union between them. If the proposal is to be accepted an act of natural faith must be made. Just as in earthly love, by faith we put our hand in the hand of God and say, "Yes, I accept your proposal. I am willing to trust myself completely to you. I do not know what the future holds, but I love you enough to surrender my whole life into your hands. I give you permission to do anything you want with me. I no longer choose to lead my own, selfish life. I want to live your life, to share everything you have; to see things as you see them; to love others as you love them; to live as you live. I commit my future destiny completely to you."

At Baptism, the first feeble response of faith is made to God. Just as a man and woman exchange their vows of marriage; just as God and the people of God exchanged their promises of love at Mt. Sinai—so the baptismal promises are the exchange of vows between God and ourselves at the beginning of our life of faith. Most of us little realize what we are promising when first baptized. However, God asks only a response that is proportionate to our ability at the time. As we mature, our commitment to God should become more and more generous. Each time we renew our baptismal vows, God's helping grace will enable us to take another step toward the total incarnation of our being with that of God. If we do our part in the growth toward natural and supernatural wholeness, the rate of our increase in faith will become considerably swifter as the years of life progress. Our first mature commitment of faith usually takes place around the age of twenty. By the time we are forty years of age we should be experiencing a tremendous increase of faith every year. If we are unaware of any growth in our faith, year after year, we should give serious consideration to the situation of our life. It does not necessarily mean that something is wrong, but the presumption is that somewhere we need to make some changes. It would be wise not to depend merely upon our own judgment in such a serious matter as faith. An experienced spiritual director should be able to diagnose the problem and suggest suitable remedies.

Because faith is a participation in the Incarnation of

Christ, it brings about profound changes in our whole being. Our intellects are given new powers to understand so that we have insights into the mysteries of God. The voice of our conscience becomes the voice of God, revealing to us God's secret desires, counseling us what to say and do on any given occasion. We are able to recognize the hand of God in the events of our own life and perhaps the lives of others. We are given the power to judge according to God's standards and to make the right decisions in accord with his will for us. Those who live the life of faith live in a new world— the supernatural world of grace. Having committed ourselves into the hands of God, everything will appear differently from what it did when we judged things purely from an earthly point of view. It is like receiving a supernatural Extra Sensory Perception. We see things we never saw in the past, although we may have been looking at these same things all our lives. By faith we attain a new and higher standpoint from which to judge reality.

Standing on the outside looking in, the world of faith is filled with darkness. The first steps of faith are carried out in total blindness as we surrender ourselves to God without knowing what is ahead of us. However, as we progress in faith, we begin to realize that the really blind people are those outside. Original sin darkened our intellects so that without faith, we wander about the world like blind men. Like Bartimeus, we hear the noise of a crowd passing and we inquire what this may be. "And they told him that Jesus of Nazareth was passing by. And he cried out, saying, 'Jesus, Son of David, have mercy on me.' Jesus asked him, 'What would you have me do for thee?' And he said, 'Lord, that I may see.' And Jesus said to him, 'Receive thy sight, thy faith has saved thee' " (Lk 18:37-42).

Jesus Christ is present in the Church today. In each

sacrament we receive, Jesus of Nazareth passes by. If we have the same desire to see that the blind beggar Bartimeus had, Jesus will touch us in the sacrament and we will suddenly begin to see everything through the eyes of Christ. It is not enough to make just one act of faith. Since faith is capable of unlimited increase, we should renew our faith each time we receive a sacrament and especially during holy Mass each Sunday or weekday. We should prepare for the commitment we make during the Liturgy by studying the beautiful examples of faith given us in Sacred Scripture. With Samuel we should say many times each day, "Speak, Lord, for thy servant heareth" (I S 3:10). With Isaia we should offer ourselves generously to the work of God as we arise each day, "Here I am, send me" (Is 6:8). With St. Paul, let us inquire again and again of God, "Lord, what wilt thou have me do?" (Acts 9:6). With the Blessed Virgin Mary at the Incarnation, let us keep our hearts and souls constantly open to God's grace, "Behold the handmaid of the Lord, be it done to me according to thy word" (Lk 1:38).

In the third aeon we will no longer have any need of faith. In the New Jerusalem the streets will be paved with the pure gold of supernatural charity (Ap 21:21). As long as we remain in our present condition, faith and hope are essential to any relationship of love with God. They form the necessary foundation for charity and together these three virtues comprise the response of supernatural love which we give to God's call of grace. Both the individual and the whole community of God's holy people must make these commitments. They should be especially made when we are united to our brethren during the liturgy. Again and again during the different feasts of the liturgical year, we should join ourselves to Christ in offering to the heavenly Father a perfect service of faith, hope and charity.

X

Finding Hope
through the Liturgy

What would we do without hope? It is hope that fills us with enthusiasm for the future and helps us to overcome present difficulties. Hope brings joy, peace, confidence and courage as we struggle with our day-to-day problems. By giving us a goal both attainable and attractive, hope furnishes the motivation to keep us moving forward. Men who are filled with hope for the future, remain young in spirit, open to new ideas and possessed of an elasticity that enables them to keep growing in perfection. Without hope, our whole life becomes gloomy and sterile. We are filled with discouragement and lacking in energy to do anything about it. When hope is lacking, fear and cowardice take possession of a person.

Christian hope is the supernatural incarnation of natural courage. By means of God's grace, a man of faith is able to make this second response of love to God's call. The virtue of hope is totally dependent upon a previous commitment of faith. Having taken this first step of faith, we need hope to keep us going. Through hope we are able to transcend time and live by anticipation in the future Kingdom of God. It is especially during our participation in the Liturgy of the Church that we enter at least for a moment the life of the third aeon. The glorified Body of Christ that we receive in the Eucharist is a substantial piece of this future kingdom now present in the second aeon. This liturgical preview of coming attractions is experienced under the veil of faith; therefore, it is considerably less than the face to face vision of God after death or the direct experiences of the Last Day. Nevertheless, the liturgical worship of the Christian Community is a real anticipation of life in the New Jerusalem. The degree of our realization of this will be in proportion to our faith.

The Church today stands on the border that separates the second from the third aeon. During the liturgy we are able to make contact with the glorified Body of Christ. In the Service of the Word, the glorified Christ speaks to us through the Scripture lessons and the homily of the priest. We are able to speak directly to Him and offer the gift of ourselves through Christ to the Father. In the Eucharist we are nourished with the body of the resurrected Christ. By means of symbols we are able to experience something of the splendor, glory and beauty of Christ's Kingdom of the Last Day. During the course of the Liturgical Year not only do we relive the events of the life of Christ in Galilee and Jerusalem, but we anticipate the life of the whole Body of Christ forever in the New Jerusalem.

During the liturgy, our goal of the third aeon becomes present. If we have the faith to accept this, the Mass and the Sacraments become for us tremendous sources of courage and strength. If the liturgy is properly celebrated by priest and people, those present will receive special graces to overcome discouragement. First of all, we will become keenly aware of our union with the rest of the community of God's people. We will realize that we do not have to fight the battles of life alone, but we have many brethren to help us. We will also have an experience of personal encounter with

Jesus Christ during the high points of the liturgical service. Christ will come to us and join forces with us in the battles of life. We will be lifted up by the Holy Spirit as a result of our participation in the liturgy and will benefit from a generous outpouring of the gifts of the Spirit. When we leave the liturgical worship we will carry with us a profound conviction that we have at last been able to satisfy the infinite debt that we owe the heavenly Father. Through Christ and in union with the Holy Spirit and our brethren, we will have offered a perfect gift to the Father.

None of these wonderful things are accomplished without effort on our part. Many things are required to make a fine liturgical celebration. It helps if our bodies and minds are well rested and alert, capable of living for a time on the high personal level required during liturgical worship. However, grace and the enthusiasm of the community can often overcome our physical lethargy. Both priest and people need to be well prepared intellectually and psychologically through study and meditation on the mysteries about to be celebrated. The actual service needs to be carried out in a sincere, reverent and meaningful way so that the words, actions and symbols are readily understandable to all. The celebrant and people need to be sufficiently familiar with the mechanics of the service that these do not become a distraction to them, but rather the instrument to make contact with the glorified life of Christ. Each person should be ready to make a total commitment of himself in faith and love to the Father through Christ and in union with the Holy Spirit.

It should be the aim of everyone in the community of worshipers to make the liturgy a communal endeavor. Individuals should sacrifice their own personal desires about the way they like to pray during the service. All should join together in singing and praying, according to the particular functions of each member of the group. Everyone should be conscious of the fact that the whole liturgical service is a community work, from beginning to end. Sacrificing personal tastes, we should aim to make it a community experience of union with Christ.

Every covenant of love that God has made with man has been a community covenant. The Old Testament was made with Abraham and his descendants. In all these pacts of love God has insisted that the whole community of the people should renew the covenant with God on certain occasions set by God himself. In the Old Testament there were certain festival days each year when all the people of God gathered around the Ark of the Covenant or in the Temple and renewed their promises to God. On the Sabbath smaller groups of the family of God gathered in the synagogue for a further renewal of their covenant with God. In the New Testament, Christians are called upon to gather around the Altar of the Lord at least once each week on the Lord's Day and there to renew their covenant of love with the Father. This is the primary reason for our assisting at the Liturgy of the Mass each Sunday. We come here at the command of Christ, our Leader, to renew our promises of love and faithfulness to the Father through Christ. We are expected to come as a community—the new family of God, the Church and the parish of which we are members. Together with our brethren we renew our covenant with the heavenly Father.

While at Mass we listen attentively to the reading and the explanation of God's Word. It is here that we should find God's instructions for the coming days and weeks. Together with the leaders of our community we make known our needs and petitions to the Lord. Then we make a solemn offering of our gifts of love, through Jesus our Brother, to the Father. Christ takes our gifts, transforms them at the Consecration and unites them to the precious gift of his own Body and Blood. Then together, Christ and all the faithful, united through the Holy Spirit, offer their most worthy gift of love and loyalty and obedience to God the Father. Now it is God's turn to renew his promises of love for us. It is a part of his covenant with us to assure us of his loyalty and faithfulness to his holy people. He promises to take care of us, to give us all the grace we need to reach his Kingdom on the Last Day. As a visible sign of this love, the heavenly Father gives us the glorified Body of Christ in the Eucharist. He insists that we should take this symbol of his love and eat it, uniting it most intimately to ourselves.

Coming forth from our Sunday Mass, we should be filled with the spirit of God himself. We need no longer be afraid of the world, of ourselves, of others, not even of God. We should have the bold spirit of conquerors, ready to go forth and do battle with all the forces of evil and overcome them. We are now ready to tackle the problems of life with renewed vigor. We should be filled with the highest hopes of victory, since we carry within us Jesus Christ the conqueror of sin, of death, of Satan and of hell itself. There will be moments in our life when we feel tired and weak, when temptations threaten to overwhelm us. If we will only think back to last Sunday's Mass or forward to next Sunday's Mass, we shall find the hope necessary to keep going ahead. For those who are fortunate enough to assist at daily Mass, there is even less reason for discouragement in the face of the difficulties of living. Throughout the day we carry within us the spirit of the triumphal Christ. Throughout the night we can look forward to an encounter with the victorious Christ at the beginning of another new day.

The liturgy of the Mass should always fill us with joy. There are times during the year when it is proper to emphasize the sufferings and death of Christ. But even these Masses insist upon the joys of the resurrection that will soon follow. The whole Christian religion is one of triumph and victory, not of sadness and defeat. If the liturgy is celebrated as it should be, the people will come forth from each Mass filled with joy and hope for the future. While at Mass we may be conscious of the fact that we are still pilgrims and exiles, making the long desert journey to the promised land. Like the early Christians, we will look forward with eager longing for the Second Coming of Christ when he will banish all evil and sadness from the earth. At the same time, there will be no doubt about the final outcome since each Mass celebrates the victory already accomplished by Jesus Christ.

Once we understand the purpose and meaning of the liturgy and participate in it fully, Christian hope will be an ever-present reality for us. The past events of our redemption and salvation are made present at Mass and the future goal of God's Kingdom is anticipated. Through the power of this hope, all our fears are conquered and we can go forward with joy and enthusiasm to whatever God has in store for us. Having made our commitment of faith, the virtue of hope keeps us going on the road with full speed ahead until we arrive at our destination of perfect love. All the sacraments give us hope, but the Mass and the Eucharist are its greatest source. It is the present tense of the verb that is used in the promise of the Eucharist, "He who eats my flesh and drinks my blood *has* life everlasting and I will raise him up on the Last Day" (Jn 6:55).

XI

Learning Charity
through Christ

On the night of the Last Supper, our Blessed Lord reminded
us, "If you love me, keep my commandments" (Jn 14:15).
In any covenant of love it is presumed that each party will
do all in his power to please the beloved. In each covenant
of love into which God has entered with men, there have
been certain requirements to be fulfilled by man in order to
please God. On Mt. Sinai he revealed to Moses the commandments that the Hebrews were to keep in order to be his
chosen people. There followed an exchange of promises
between God and the assembly of the elect which was irrevocably sealed in blood. God promised to be faithful to his
chosen people, to protect them from their enemies, to bring
them to the promised land and to help them gain possession
of it. The assembly of the chosen ones promised to show
their love for him by obeying his commandments. Because
the Jews were still in an early stage of culture, the commandments of the Old Testament were limited to minimum
requirements and worded in a negative way. This was the
most God could expect at this time.

With the coming of Christ, another covenant of love
was made between the heavenly Father and the Christian
Community. New promises were exchanged between God

and the new family of his people. This exchange of vows was sealed in the blood of Christ upon the cross. Not only did the God-man promise to bring the people to the Kingdom of God on the Last Day, he promised to lay down his life for them. "Greater love than this, no one has, that one lay down his life for his friends" (Jn 15:13). Likewise, the people of God are expected to do considerably more than the chosen people of the Old Testament. "A new commandment I give you, that you love one another; that as I have loved you, you also love one another" (Jn 13:34). As Christians, the standard by which we must measure our love for our neighbor is the unlimited love which Christ Jesus has for us.

The commitment of faith is the beginning of our response of love to God's call of grace in the New Testament. To persevere in our love we make use of Christian hope to give us the courage to keep progressing towards our goal of perfect union with God. The virtue of Christian charity is the perfection and completion of the love that we have been commanded by Christ to have and to give to others. This fullness of love is not only to be given to God, but also to our brethren. "As long as you did it for one of these, the least of my brethren, you did it for me" (Mt 25:40). Until the coming of Christ, it was impossible for God to ask this kind of love from us. Love is something that we can learn only through the actual experience of being loved by another person. It was necessary that Christ give us the example of the love that he expected of us, his brethren. Charity, therefore, is an exclusively Christian virtue. Only those who possess Christian faith and hope are able to practice it.

Let no one imagine that it is easy to practice Christian charity. Besides the special helping grace from God, there is need of great effort on our part to rise to this supernatural level of love. Charity is the incarnation of the natural virtue of love and to attain it requires free consent and cooperation of both God and ourselves. Through the sacraments we are given the necessary grace from God to attain this new standard of love—Christ's love for us. If we cooperate with the grace of faith and hope that comes to us through the liturgy, we should have many wonderful experiences of the love of Jesus Christ for us. As one Christian Feast succeeds another and as one liturgical year follows another, the community of God's chosen people should have many encounters of love with the God-man, Jesus Christ. Through our participation in the actions of the Mystical Body of Christ from day to day, we will get to know from first-hand experience what it means to be loved by God in human form.

A life-time of effort on our part is necessary in order to attain the degree of love which the New Covenant of Christ requires. This should be considered a challenge rather than a reason for discouragement. In these present "between-times," before the Second Coming of Christ, we are to prepare ourselves for the third aeon. The full life only begins on the Last Day when Christ will establish his permanent Kingdom on earth. We are not expected at present to love others with the same unlimited love that Christ gives us. However, we are expected to work hard to cooperate with the graces of God that are given us and to advance each day a step nearer to the fullness of supernatural love. As long as we keep progressing toward perfect love, we should be happy. We need only be concerned when, year after year, we can see no real improvement in the manner of our loving God and others. Love is a living thing and so never remains the same. If it is not advancing, we can be sure that somewhere down deep in our being, it is decaying and dying.

What can we do to make sure that our love for God

and our brethren becomes more Christ-like? If our knowledge and love of Christ grows a little each day, then both consciously and unconsciously our love for others will more and more resemble the love of Christ. It is impossible to love another sincerely and deeply without at the same time imitating him. If therefore we desire to fulfill our part of the New Covenant, we need to progress through all four steps of love in our relationship with Christ. Jesus Christ must become the focal point of everything in our life. His Incarnation is the origin of all the graces that have come to us from the Father. It is through him in the Liturgy that we make our return of love and service to the Father. Through union with Christ in the sacraments and in his Mystical Body, we attain here on earth the highest possible union with God.

The first step in loving Christ is getting to know all about him. We must study and meditate upon every detail of his life until we come to know him as a real person and not just as a book. Through a daily effort on our part, it is possible rather quickly for the marvelous personality of Christ to come to life for us. We will find ourselves greatly attracted to him, absorbed by every slightest detail of his character. We will read everything we can find, if it promises to give us some new insight into his human and divine natures. After a while, we will come to have our favorite authors who in our opinion seem to have best captured the wonderful personality of Jesus. We will love to read their books again and again, meditating long afterwards on the picture they have given us of Christ. However, we will turn more and more to the four Gospels, because by now we know enough about the character of Christ to read and interpret ourselves the deeper meanings of his words and actions. We will enjoy comparing the texts of Matthew, Mark, Luke and John in a

Harmony of the Gospels, picking out every detail given by one or the other evangelists. The Gospels become for us the love-letters from our beloved Christ; we want to read them again and again, each time with greater comprehension than in previous readings. Once caught by the magnetic personality of Jesus, there is little danger that we will forsake him.

While growing in the understanding and appreciation of Christ, without realizing it, we will begin to make comparisons between his character and our own. The greater the contrast between the way Christ spoke and acted and our behavior, the more we will realize the need of change on our part. This is the second step of love where we desire to open ourselves to the beloved so that he may know us as we really are. We don't want to hide anything from him or from ourselves. Seeing the honesty and straight-forwardness of Christ, we will want to imitate his frankness and sincerity. Through learning to know Christ, we will learn to know ourselves and to recognize what we need to do in order to be like him.

The third step of love called benevolence will also have been growing apace with our increased knowledge of Christ. Our hearts go out instinctively towards an object that the intellect presents as being good. Therefore, every step in our knowledge of the infinite goodness of Christ will result in an increased desire to please and imitate him. Our love for Christ will cause us to study how he served others, so that we can do likewise. We will take seriously his command to love others as he loves us and our lives will begin to grow in unselfish service for others.

The desire for union with Christ will make us long for that ultimate union with him in the Kingdom of God. We will not be content to wait so long but will seek every opportunity to become one with him here and now, looking forward with eager longing to every participation in the liturgy, especially holy Mass. Having studied the Word of God in the Gospels, we will want to eat of this Word made flesh in the Eucharist. Our Eucharistic union will in turn make us want to extend this union with Christ through charity for our brethren, the members of his Mystical Body.

Another way of continuing the union with Christ is through loving conversation with him, either in the presence of the Blessed Sacrament or anywhere during the day. Knowing that we carry him within us through grace, we will find great joy and satisfaction in speaking to him whenever we are alone. When in the presence of others, our faith will tell us that Jesus is likewise dwelling within them; thus we are able to show our reverence and love for our Brother Christ by the respect and service we give to his brethren. Here is one friend that we never need be afraid of losing. "Behold I am with you all days, even unto the consummation of the world" (Mt 28:20). "I will not leave you orphans; I will come to you. . . . In that day you will know that I am in my Father, you in me and I in you. . . . He who loves me will be loved by my Father and I will love him and manifest myself to him" (Jn 14:18-21).

XII

The New Commandments of Christ

In the Old Testament, God was content with a minimum compliance to the ten commandments, but with the coming of Christ much more is expected. "You therefore are to be perfect, even as your heavenly Father is perfect" (Mt 6:48). We are to model our life and service upon the life and actions of Jesus Christ. We are to submit our whole being to the heavenly Father as did Christ. In the Sermon on the Mount we are given the new commandments required for the New Testament. God, through Moses, asked the people of the Old Testament to promise obedience to the commandments of Mt. Sinai; likewise, Christ on another mountain in Galilee asked his disciples to live according to the new law of perfection found in the Gospels. The obligations of Christian charity are often called counsels instead of commandments to emphasize the fact that God wants them to be motivated by love rather than fear. The Sermon on the Mount and the counsels of perfection in the Gospels are addressed to all Christians and not merely to priests and religious. There is no place for fence-sitters or those who choose to be mediocre in the Kingdom of Christ. When our love is truly sincere, half-measures are impossible in our commitment to Christ. "Thou shalt love the Lord thy God with thy *whole* heart, with thy *whole* soul, with thy *whole* strength and with thy *whole* mind" (Lk 10:27).

To appreciate how exceedingly higher are the requirements of love from Christians than from those of the Old Testament, it is useful to compare the Mosaic Commandments with the Gospel counsels in the Sermon on the Mount. God commanded the Israelites not to worship false gods; we are commanded to love the Father with the love of Christ. The Old Testament forbade cursing; the New Testament urges a constant, loving discourse with God in prayer. The primary obligation for the Jews on the Sabbath was to refrain from work. We are commanded to use our Sunday leisure to perform the work of love called the Eucharist and to carry out other works of charity toward our brethren. Moses told the Jews not to dishonor their parents; we are expected to show an unlimited love and service for our heavenly Father and our brethren. The Old Law demanded that we do not kill; Christian charity requires us to lay down our lives for others. Moses permitted divorce but forbade adultery; Christians are expected to be united in the most intimate bonds of natural and supernatural love with all the people of God. The commandments of Mt. Sinai forbade stealing; Christ commands us, "go, sell whatever you have and give to the poor" (Mk 10:21). The Jews were forbidden to lie; the New Law expects of us the same openness and honesty as we see in Christ. "Learn of me for I am meek and humble of heart" (Mt 11:29). The Israelites were told not to covet their neighbor's wife or goods; we are told to be willing to give away everything in our love for others.

As Christians, our model in loving and serving is Christ. The imitation of his heroic charity is possible through the abundant grace of God. Christ, having commanded these things, will most certainly give us the means to perform them. However, the accomplishment of Christian charity will not automatically follow from the bestowal of grace. We must cooperate in order to reach this heroic level of charity expected of us. This high level is made clear to us in the eight beatitudes which form the Magna Carta of the Sermon on the Mount and the whole new age introduced by Jesus Christ.

Blessed Are the Poor in Spirit for Theirs Is the Kingdom of Heaven

The poor in spirit are those who are keenly aware of their lack of goodness. This implies a high degree of self-knowledge, which comes only to those who are able to face up to themselves as they really are in God's sight. This poverty of spirit gives them a wonderful freedom from pride and vanity and is the necessary preparation for any union with God. Having emptied their souls of excessive preoccupation with themselves, they are now open to the graces of God. Being aware of their lack of goodness, they become beggars of the Holy Spirit for the needed supernatural help. Only those humble enough to realize their own poverty are able to find room in their hearts for Christ. Having opened their hearts to Christ's love, they are assured in this beatitude that God will give them his kingdom of grace. This possession of God's kingdom will begin already in this second aeon—"theirs *is* the kingdom of heaven."

Blessed Are the Meek for They Shall Possess the Earth

Meekness here means sensitivity to everything of God's— his will, his love, his spirit. Just as the strings of a sensitive violin vibrate the same notes that are struck upon a nearby piano, so the meek person responds instantly to every indication of God's will. This is the meekness of Christ—"I do always the things that are pleasing to my Father" (Jn 8:29).

To attain this meekness our minds and hearts must be completely open to truth, both natural and supernatural. We must be able to distinguish the inner voice of God's Spirit from the destructive voice of our egocentricity. We need to free ourselves from the blindness and distractions created by selfish attachments to creatures. Through loving Christ and others we will make our hearts tender and susceptible to the least movement of God's love. To attain this sensitivity we must overcome our inhibitions and repressions and cultivate a delicate response to every manifestation of truth and love. Instead of being enslaved to the things of the earth, the meek have only one master—Christ, the God-man. Independent of the world, they are the only persons capable of being true masters and possessors of the earth.

Blessed Are They Who Mourn for They Shall Be Comforted

When our Blessed Lord drew near to Jerusalem on his last journey, he wept over the city. "If thou hadst known, in this thy day, the things that are for thy peace. But now they are hidden from thy eyes" (Lk 19:42). Anyone who is filled with the charity of Christ will sincerely mourn at the sight of evil and the suffering that inevitably follows. Our anguish of spirit must be an honest suffering that comes from love and not from mere anger at ourselves or others. Suffering motivated by love deepens and broadens our whole personality and the cross becomes a stepping stone to a higher level of existence. By means of God's helping graces our mourning becomes an experience of incarnation that lifts us up into a greater union with God, and in the possession of this greater charity we find a deep comfort. Our faith enables us to see the value of suffering and Christian hope gives us here and now a joyful anticipation of the future good.

Blessed Are They Who Hunger and Thirst for Justice for They Shall Be Satisfied

If we love Christ, we will have something of his intense longing for justice, both natural and supernatural. Our desire to see that everyone is given what is due to him will be similar to the craving of a starving man in search of food. We will want to see God's desires fulfilled on earth very much as a man dying of thirst longs for water. We will experience no peace within ourselves unless we are continually striving with every fiber of our being to see that justice is done to everyone. This means, first of all, a desire to see that God is given the honor, the love, and the service that is due to him. In our desire for the coming of God's kingdom we will go to any extreme to do our part to accomplish it, both in ourselves and in others. As long as there is any injustice anywhere in the world, we will not be satisfied until it has been righted. Our Lord tells us that it is a great blessing to possess this intense craving for justice. He promises that if we persevere in our desires and implement them as best we can by our actions, then surely, we will live to see justice accomplished. God never gives us a desire without, at the same time, making available the means to fulfill it. If we are willing to pay the price for justice, we shall surely be satisfied. The price that Christ paid was death on Calvary; if we wish to be his disciples, we will need to endure much violence before our thirst for justice is quenched.

Blessed Are the Merciful for They Shall Obtain Mercy

Our mercy to our neighbor is similar to meekness toward God. The meek possess the earth while the merciful give it away to their brethren. If we give, we will receive, since love is never lost by being shared but instead it is multiplied. Meekness makes us sensitive to the wants of God; mercy renders us sensitive to the needs of our neighbor. To do this we have to overcome our egotism that blinds us to the needs of everyone except ourselves. With understanding and sympathy we learn to feel the calamities endured by others as though they were our own. Through the love of Christ we identify ourselves as completely as possible with our brethren, and through grace reach the point of saying with Christ, "what you do to one of these, the least of my brethren, you do unto me." To have attained this identity of love with our neighbor is proof of a similar identity of love with Christ. Through mercy we share all that we have with others; at the same time we merit a share in all the possessions of Christ and our brethren. To give mercy is to receive it.

Blessed Are the Clean of Heart for They Shall See God

The purity of heart in the Sermon on the Mount means considerably more than sexual chastity. Negatively, it is the absence of egocentricity; positively, it is the power to see God and good everywhere we look. "For the pure, all things are pure" (Tit 1:15). Instead of seeing evil, the pure of heart see the possibilities of good in everyone and every event. A pure heart is a creative heart, capable of bringing good out of everything, even out of evil. "For those who love God, all things work together unto good" (Rom 8:28).

Purity of heart is not an easy process during this second aeon. We must first work hard to purify our own lives of all evil; only then will we be able to see with a clear eye the potential for good in others. To see God in a sinner may mean to see the wonderful capacity for good in that person. To bring forth this good, will require great pains of labor. However, if we have succeeded through patient suffering to transform the evil in ourselves into good; then we will have gained the proficiency to help our brethren do likewise. To attain purity of heart we will need many graces from God and the first grace for which to ask is the light to see the possibilities for good in each of our faults. With this knowledge, we will be able to face up to the full truth about ourselves without anger, denial or discouragement—only determination to turn the mistakes of the past into future good.

Blessed Are the Peacemakers for They Shall Be Called Children of God

Peace is the tranquility of order—when everyone and everything is in its proper place, we have peace. It is our task as disciples of Christ to help establish peace between God and man, man and man, grace and nature, individual and community, body and soul. There is no greater power given to us than the power to bring peace and love and joy between God and man or between man and man. Those who share with Christ in this task of peace-making will be the ones who most directly work to prepare this earth for the third aeon. Peace will never be attained by compromise or cowardice. It will be found only through the incarnation of everything natural into the supernatural level of grace. In this sense a peacemaker is a co-creator with God in building the kingdom of the renewed creation. For those who are successful in this difficult task of peacemaking, there is great danger of pride; therefore we must accept our place as children of God and be mindful that all our good comes from our heavenly Father.

Blessed Are They Who Suffer Persecution for Justice's Sake for Theirs Is the Kingdom of Heaven

Not every persecution is a blessing but only that which results from our efforts to please God and work justice. If we are successful in pleasing God, we will arouse the fury of his enemies. Those who are satisfied with their mediocrity will resist us because we disturb them. The slothful who resist all change will be unhappy because we upset their comfort and security. Egocentric persons will recognize us as an enemy and will do all in their power to destroy us. They will consider us dangerous innovators, a threat to their own peace. However, we need not fear this kind of persecution; instead of harming us, it purifies us of whatever selfishness that remains in our life and speeds up our growth in natural and supernatural wholeness. Again and again they will seek to kill us, only to find that we rise each time from the tomb more glorious than ever. Just as Christ redeemed the world through his sufferings and death, so we will continue the work of Christ's redemption through the persecutions we endure at the hands of his enemies. "For those who love God, all things work together unto good . . . for those whom he has foreknown he has also predestined to become conformed to the image of his Son" (Rom 8:28-29).

XIII

The Psychology of Sin and Temptation

Just as there were enemies of God in the garden of paradise, so there are enemies today who strive with all their might to destroy love or prevent it from spreading. It is important that we be able to recognize our adversaries, call them by their right name and know all we can about them. Satan works best in darkness; he is like a fish out of water when we expose his devious ways. What are obstacles to the working of grace when hidden, can become instruments for the increase of grace when open. Every fault is a misdirected virtue. If the energy behind a sin is used properly, it can become just as effective an instrument for good as it formerly was for evil. This work of sublimating evil into good needs the helping grace of God, which is made available in the sacraments, especially Penance and Eucharist. The transformation of faults into virtues also requires great effort on our part. The first of these is to get to know the nature of sin and temptation.

Evil is the absence of a good that should be present in a particular creature. Evil never stands alone since it is a negative thing—a deprivation of something that belongs by nature in a person or thing. We never find "pure" evil but only a mixture of evil and good. The creature in which a certain "good" is lacking will still be good in itself. This makes it possible for evil to hide behind the good, so that someone who looks only at the exterior will imagine that the whole is good. It is only by a process of study and reasoning that we are able to isolate the evil and see it as it really is. The more proficient we become at doing this, the less danger there will be from sin. "You shall know the truth and the truth shall make you free" (Jn 8:32).

All sin is a substitution of our ego as the center of our life in the place of God. If the proper order of love exists in our life, then God will be the true ruler. The power of our person was so weakened by original sin, that without grace it is impossible to make God the lord and center of our life. However, if we allow ourselves to be touched by his grace, then our whole being becomes filled with the same power and life that God himself possesses. Strengthened by him, our own person is able to become the true master of our whole life, subjecting our ego and all our other faculties to the will of God. Our ego, however, chafes under the subservient position which has been imposed upon it and often attempts to assert its freedom by rebelling against God's will. Our other faculties, irritated by the restraint being imposed upon them, often rally around the ego and encourage it to set itself up as their king. It takes much effort on our part to keep these rebellious forces under control. If we knowingly and freely consent to their wayward tendencies, we have sinned.

Once the ego has kicked over the traces and asserted its independence, there is often a short period of rejoicing in the new-found freedom. However, the ego was never created to be the sole ruler of our lives and it is incapable of keeping order within us. Other conscious and unconscious powers rebel against the ego just as it has rebelled against God. The ego may be strong enough to handle the conscious powers of intellect, memory and imagination, but it is helpless against the deeper unconscious instincts of sex, love, power and ambition. These begin to assert themselves through conscious desires which the ego may try desperately to control. However, the conscious ego finds itself powerless against the hidden and unknown unconscious; consequently, one's life becomes progressively filled with chaos and frustration. The ego may strive to reassert its stolen position as the center of our life, but instead of remedying the situation, matters become worse. Egocentricity creates a hard callousness around the heart and its ability to go outward in love. Others may try to love the sinner, but find themselves unable to penetrate the hard armor of selfishness that now encloses his whole person. Even the grace of God finds it difficult to break down this high wall that egotism has built around the heart.

Thanks to God's infinite goodness and mercy, the sinner is not abandoned to the reckless course of destruction he has chosen. Again and again, divine providence makes an opening in the hard crust of selfishness that surrounds the sinner. Frequently this opening is accomplished through some tragedy like the death of an associate, personal illness or business failure; at other times it is disgust with one's own way of life, a sense of loneliness that comes from lack of love, a feeling of frustration and lack of completion in one's life. All the possible crises that can happen in one's life are so many opportunities for a conversion to take place—a turning away from evil and a turning back to good. Very much depends upon the circumstances of one's life at the time of these crises. If the sinner makes contact with another person who has overcome his egocentricity and who truly loves, this will be a wonderful inspiration to encourage the sinful person to do likewise. This encounter with love can be experienced through reading a book—the Gospels, the life of a saint, etc., as well as first-hand from a living person. Perhaps it is the memory of some love received in the past from a parent, a teacher or a friend. Since God does not will the death of a sinner, but that he be converted and live, we are sure that in times of crisis everyone will be given the opportunity to experience love in one form or another.

The more hardened the sinner, the more love and grace required to help him overcome the hostility to God that he has allowed to develop in his soul. Before making the deliberate choice to reject God's will, he must convince himself that God does not really love him. He must conjure up the false notion that God is in some way evil and an enemy to his best interests. The more often and deliberately one sins, the deeper will become this hostility to God. This hatred for God can be carried over from one generation to another, so that we grow up unconsciously resenting our need of obeying God's commandments and submitting to his will. We feel that God hinders our freedom and we long to assert our independence of him and his laws. The greatest danger is present when this hostility is unconscious while consciously we seem to be perfectly submissive to God's will. We are considerably safer when our hostility and resentment towards God is out in the open so that we can do something about it.

At least half of the battle in overcoming sin is to recognize the evil as it actually exists in our souls. There are very few really malicious persons who deliberately choose evil as evil. Usually we are more or less duped into sinning, surrendering to the temptation without fully realizing what we are doing. At first there is only a partial consent to some imperfection or sin. There may follow a whole series of semi-deliberate sins with the malice getting progressively worse. If the trend is not halted, it can eventually lead to the deliberate plunge into mortal sin with one's eyes fully open. All of this can be avoided if we face the evil within us while it is still small. We should acknowledge each day the seeds of evil that present themselves so that we are able to conquer them before they grow into giant trees.

It takes a lifetime of effort to bring to the surface our unconscious evil tendencies and we must not be in too big a hurry to uncover all this evil hidden within our being. If it were exposed at one time, the shock would perhaps be so great that we would be filled with despair. It is God's will that we progress a little each day, according to the light that we are given. "Do not be anxious about tomorrow, for tomorrow will have anxieties of its own. Sufficient for the day is its own trouble" (Mt 6:34). If we cooperate each day with God's graces we can hope to have completed the work of purification by the moment of our death.

It is a great help if we find friends who can help us to discern the evil tendencies within us. If they can also teach us to sublimate and transform these wayward tendencies into good, then we will find ourselves exceedingly blessed. The greatest of these blessings will be to have a wise and experienced spiritual director who will help us find our way out of the darkness of evil into the kingdom of grace. Especially at first, we should not trust our own judgment in these matters. Under the guidance of a director who is familiar with the ways of nature as well as the ways of grace, we will grow in our ability to see ourselves as we really are. As we grow in natural maturity and sanctity, we will need less outside direction, except during the time of a new crisis in our life. In the beginning we should be satisfied to transform one fault each year into a virtue; but with each passing year, we should experience more frequent victories.

We must not allow ourselves to be led astray by the mere external symptoms of evil. Just as a headache indicates trouble somewhere in the interior of our body, so outward faults are usually indications of much deeper and unconscious evils. The most obvious example of this is the matter of temptations against chastity. In most instances, the real problem is not sex but the lack of a proper, selfless love for others. If one has problems with unchaste temptations, it is not enough to struggle against them directly: one should try to discover where the basic drive of love in the depths of his being has gone astray. If the direction of love can be changed so that it goes outward to others and is not bent backward upon oneself, the temptations against chastity will disappear of their own accord.

Most temptations proceed from one or another form of egocentricity. An example of this is found in temptations against faith. The real problem here is usually a lack of generosity in our total commitment to God. The particular doubts against an article of faith are often an attempt of the unconscious to awaken in us the realization that something is wrong in our basic relationship toward God. Sexual temptations indicate the lack of a proper unselfish love for our neighbor; temptations against faith suggest the lack of a mature and healthy attitude towards God. If we succeed in straightening out the four elemental desires of love and keep the proper order among the objects of our love, usually the temptations subside.

It is usually a mistake to try directly to repress a temptation when it becomes conscious. It is like trying to stop up a vein of water that suddenly springs up in the middle of a field. This does not really stop the flow of water, but drives it underground until the whole field is a swamp. It is impossible to destroy a spiritual energy within us. We can only change its direction toward a good object rather than a bad one. We should not be morbidly afraid of a temptation but recognize it for what it really is—energy for good that has gone astray. Instead of trying to destroy the energy we must struggle with it and find a legitimate outlet in love. Every problem of evil is in some way connected with love and love is usually difficult to practice here on earth. It is only by a life-long struggle and cooperation with God's graces that we will succeed in overcoming the effects of past sins and reach perfect love.

Everything of the past, including our deliberate sins, can be turned into instruments of good. Everything of the present and future, including the greatest possible temptations, can all be used to mature and sanctify us, provided we are sincere and make use of God's grace. Sometimes they are advance signs that something is wrong in our relationships with God and others. At another time, these temptations are indications that God is calling us to a higher degree of love than what we have given him in the past. God may be pleased with what we have done and now wants to lead us to a higher mansion of grace. Regardless of the cause, every temptation can serve the worthy purpose of purifying us of egotism and preparing us for perfect union with God. These struggles with our evil tendencies are our Way of the Cross which takes us across the hill of Calvary to the resurrection of a new life of grace. Temptations do not automatically cease when we work hard to grow in natural and supernatural wholeness. A lifetime cooperation with God's helping graces is required to become a saint, but as long as we have some real assurance that we are on the right road, we should not mind how long or difficult that road may be.

XIV

The Abuse of Love

Pharisaism

In our relationship with God, probably the most frequent abuse of love is to treat God as a thing rather than a person. This was the sin of the Pharisees whom our Lord condemned so often and so strongly. Instead of making religion a personal relationship of love, the Pharisees made it a business deal—I will give God these things, if he will give me salvation. No matter how much we give God, he is not satisfied unless we give him ourselves in wholehearted love. Religion is not a question of the quantity of external actions and things that we can offer God; rather it is the quality and intensity of the commitment of love that we are willing to make to him. The Pharisee was unwilling to make this surrender of his whole person in love; therefore, he tried to satisfy his religious obligations by a scrupulous adherence to the external requirements of God's laws. He occupied himself with the accidental details and formalities of worship, while neglecting the inner spirit of a devoted love. The personal relationship of Christ to his Father was a constant witness against the absence of love in the religion of the Pharisees. Unwilling to rid themselves of their Pharisaism, they turned in hatred upon Christ and destroyed him.

Throughout the centuries of Christianity, the evil of Pharisaism has continued to haunt the lives of Christians who were unwilling or unable to love God in a personal way. It is so much easier to dispose of our religious obligations when it is a matter of fulfilling the mere letter of the law. To love a person is a very difficult and demanding work; when this person is an invisible God, the task of loving becomes almost insurmountable. Thanks to God's constant helping grace and thanks to the coming of God in human flesh, the task of having a personal love for God is always possible. The first step to attain the proper relationship of love is to become aware of how much the spirit of the Pharisees has pervaded our own religious practices. Are we excessively preoccupied with the number and quantity of our prayers, with the rubrics and other accidentals of worship? Is our attitude the juridical attitude of the Pharisees or the pastoral attitude of Christ? Are we more concerned with laws or with persons? Are we too literal in stressing conformity to the letter of the law to the neglect of a personal love for the heavenly Father? If we love God as we should, we will find a place for all these things, but never will we allow them to take precedence over the task of attaining a love for God.

Pride

At the origin of the Pharisees' problem was pride, which St. Thomas Aquinas says is the beginning of all abuses of love. He defines pride as the exaggerated love of one's own excellence to the extent that a certain contempt of God results. The greatest contempt we can have for God is to treat him as a thing rather than a person. This frequently occurs when we are wrapped up in ourselves and our own interests and have no time to be concerned personally about anyone else, God included. We treat everyone, even God, as something to be used for our own advantage or amusement. The only persons we take seriously are ourselves and, in due time, this leads to some form of self-idolatry. Pride is an exaggeration of the proper estimation we should have of the good within us. The first step in overcoming pride is to recognize the many devious forms it takes in our life. How do we treat others, both God and our brethren? Do we strive to let our hearts go out to them in love and service or do we use them for our own benefit? Remembering how our Lord identified himself with our brethren, we must realize that any contempt we show for other human beings is likewise showing contempt for God.

Vanity

Not only do we abuse love by showing contempt for our neighbors, we are also guilty of abuse when we exaggerate the importance of the good opinion of our neighbors. This is called vanity, which is an excessive desire for the approval of others. Lacking a sense of inner security, the vain person becomes a slave to human respect. He will go to almost any extreme to obtain praise and honor from others. The desire to please one's fellow-men becomes more important than the desire to please God. A vain man makes all his judgments in the light of what other people will think, especially those people upon whom he depends in one way or another. Lacking confidence in ourselves, we become slaves to public opinion. Because vanity is such a childish fault, most adults are unwilling to face up to the extent that it motivates their actions. The ability to conceal it usually succeeds only in the eyes of the vain man himself. Most other people see rather quickly through the more or less crude attempts that are made to obtain praise, honor and the good opinion of others. If anyone wishes to be cured of this fault, he should start with the assumption that he has some vanity of which he is unaware. The next step is to find an honest friend who will remind him of his fault each time it appears. After that it requires a life-time of effort to bring about the proper balance in our love and respect for the desires of others. Through faith and hope in God we can gain that self-confidence and inner security that will enable us to be properly independent of the opinions of others.

Covetousness

The lack of inner peace and security shows itself in other ways besides vanity. St. Thomas Aquinas puts all these under the word covetousness which he claims is the root of all sins. He defines covetousness as the exaggerated love of creatures. The covetous person has such an overwhelming desire for the things of this world that he will go to any extreme to obtain them. Like Eve in the garden of paradise, he is not satisfied with what he now possesses; so he allows himself to become obsessively attracted to the temporal goods of money, property, food, drink, pleasure, etc. It is possible to turn from the proper love of God only when we allow ourselves to be captivated by an excessive love for some creature of God. The more insecure we are in our possession of God, the more we feel the need of money, property, food and other temporal goods. If we surrender to these desires, gradually, imperceptibly we become enslaved to one or more of them: food, drink, tobacco, coffee, sex, clothes, nice cars, beautiful homes, fine furniture, brilliant conversation, bridge clubs, antiques, expensive vacations, travel, bank account, large property holdings, power, high office or any of a host of others.

There is place for all of these worldly things, provided we put the things of God first. The danger of covetousness is that we give lip service to God, while actually making a false god of one or more of his creatures. The first step to overcoming this slavery to the things of the world is to recognize how attracted we are to the goods of the world. Because we have grossly exaggerated their value, we feel very insecure without them. To overcome this insecurity we must take time to build up a great confidence in God. As we grow in the knowledge and love of God, our fears and anxiety about the goods of this world will lessen. If we can experience some real encounters of love with God, the attractiveness of the world will proportionately lessen.

Avarice

Of all the forms of covetousness, both Sacred Scripture (I Tim 6:10) and St. Thomas Aquinas insist that avarice is the most difficult to overcome. This is the exaggerated love of money and material things. The more insecure one feels within himself, the more he will feel the need of amassing a large quantity of wealth. Therefore, once we have faced up to the presence of avarice within our souls, the next step is to try to counteract it by increasing confidence in God. Through the love that is given and received from God, we will begin to experience a legitimate self-confidence that will enable us to break the chains of greed that enslave our souls. The more peace and inner security we feel with God, the less fear we will have of being without the necessary goods of this world.

Gluttony

Another form of covetousness is gluttony, which is the excessive desire for the pleasures of food and drink. This is particularly difficult to master because we must learn the habit of moderation, especially in the matter of food. Human nature is so constructed that it is easier to give up something entirely than it is to use it with temperance. Moderation is essential in almost everything in life; therefore, the self-control that we are able to develop in eating will enable us to practice the virtue of temperance elsewhere. For this reason, our Lord in the Gospels places fasting almost on an equal footing with prayer as a means to rid ourselves of evil. "This kind can be cast out in no way except by prayer and fasting" (Mk 9:28). Without many experiences in fasting it is often impossible to bear the necessary pain for a continual growth in maturity and sanctity. One's ability to pray and love God can ordinarily be measured by the willingness with which we renounce the pleasures of food and drink.

Lust

Closely akin to gluttony is lust; this is the exaggerated desire for the pleasures of sex. Only one who has solved the problems of sex according to his particular state of life is able to have a proper love for God, for others, for himself and for the world. An excessive fear of sex is very nearly as bad as an exaggerated love of it. The intensity of the suffering frequently required to bring it under control is exceedingly valuable in giving us a true picture of the extent of our egocentricity. During the struggle with sexual temptations we will be confronted with a thousand different aspects of our egotism. Much help from God and our fellow-men is usually needed to help us fight our way through the intricacies of sensuality to the freedom of true love. In our efforts to control the instinctive desires of sex, we must be careful not to develop a false attitude. Sex is not something evil but a power for good, provided it is used in the proper way. Married people as well as single people need to practice abstinence in this matter; otherwise, they will become enslaved to it. Everyone must learn how to unite the physical attraction to a truly spiritual and unselfish love for the other person. Sex is one of those vital energies that must never be merely repressed. Either we find a legitimate outlet for its energy by means of spiritual love or it will fill our whole life with fears, anxieties, egotism and brutality. For the celibate person this outlet must be found in a life of all-out love and service for one's brethren.

Sloth

In the efforts necessary for a life of loving service for others, another hindrance will be found in the tendency to sloth. St. Thomas Aquinas rather neatly defines this as the evil sadness that overtakes us at the prospect of the hard labor required to attain a spiritual good. Everyone of us has experienced this spiritual laziness; probably more often than we care to admit. In this second aeon, no fault is overcome, no virtue acquired, without much effort. If we do not attain the maturity and sanctity that God has destined for us, it will be due, among other things, to our sloth. This distorted love of self is particularly harmful when it concerns our religious duties. Our prayer life becomes boring, tiresome and full of distractions: a state of lukewarmness renders our whole spiritual life barren. A host of faults flow from sloth—

cowardice in the face of duty; discouragement at the effort required for virtue; resentment for those who interfere with our self-centered life; bitterness for God who asks so much of us; loss of enthusiasm for the higher values of life. A lifetime of strenuous effort is required to attain the love that is abused by sloth.

Envy

Another form of evil sadness is that which we feel toward the success of others, and it is called envy. Having an exaggerated love of ourselves, we consider the good fortune of our rivals an affront to our own feelings of superiority. This resentment is especially strong if someone apparently less talented than ourselves happens to be more successful than we have been. We experience deep pain whenever we hear others praising him and we do all in our power to depreciate him in our own judgment and often to others. If unchecked, envy turns into a hatred that may stop at nothing to destroy the reputation of the one who has outstripped us. Criticism, detraction, calumny, back-biting are some of the means used to tear down the good name of the other. Sometimes the reason for the envy is one's own lack of security or refusal to put forth all the effort expected of us. None of us should be quick to deny the presence of envy in ourselves. Most criticism of others is motivated by this false love of self. With much effort to cooperate with God's grace we can hope to transform our warped love of self into a sincere love of others.

Anger

The final form of covetousness is that of anger, which is the desire to attack violently anyone who is a threat to us. Anger can be used as a legitimate weapon against real evil. It becomes an evil enslavement when it is uncontrolled or when it is used for egotistical purposes. Frequently it is an indication of our own lack of inner peace and security. We react violently to anyone who poses a threat to the high estimate we have of our own excellence or who threatens the precarious hold we have on our possessions. At other times, anger is an attempt to repair by revenge a loss of face suffered at the hands of another. If we have a feeling of great insecurity, we will be unable to tolerate peacefully any humiliation, defeat or sign of weakness. The more lacking in inner confidence, the more we will attack the one who threatens our freedom of action. If we are afraid to attack the actual one who is a threat to us, then we will turn unreasonably to some other person, usually a helpless inferior, and vent our rage on him for some nonsensical reason.

Any number of things can arouse an evil anger in us, but in every instance it is an indication of an abuse of self-love. Usually it is something within us that is disturbing us, but we are afraid or unwilling to face up to the real problem, so we project our wrath upon some likely victim who happens to cross our path. This often is someone who has a similar fault and the presence of this person disturbs us more than he usually would, because he is an unconscious reminder of our own failures. Therefore the first step in overcoming anger is to take very seriously the things that disturb us in others and try to see whether we are actually guilty of the same or similar fault. The next step is to learn to love our "fault" in the same way that a mother might love a wayward or sick child. The fault is not all bad but is rather a misdirected virtue. Having isolated this evil tendency in ourselves, let us show the proper patience and love in transforming it into something good. With strenuous efforts on our part we will be able to turn the energy behind our anger into a powerful force of love. People with violent tempers are those who are capable of intense love, provided they will cooperate with God's graces in bringing about an incarnation within themselves.

XV

The Conversion of Evil into Good

It is not good to attempt a mere repression of an evil tendency that we find in ourselves. If it is repressed out of sight of our consciousness, it regresses into the unconscious where we no longer have any control over it. There it festers and corrupts our inner being, filling us with unhealthy fears and anxieties. The proper but more difficult procedure is to enter into combat with each of our faults until we have succeeded in transforming it into a true virtue. This is primarily a problem of learning to direct the energy behind the fault into the proper channel of love. The more powerful the evil tendency, the greater the possibilities of love that are present within us. Instead of being disturbed by grievous temptations, we should rejoice that the Lord has given us a strong character. This kind of personality is capable of immense good as well as immense evil, but it is to be preferred to a weak mind and heart that is incapable of producing results for good or for evil.

The conversion of evil into love is not an easy task and the greater one's potential for sanctity, the more difficult this work will be. It is a job that is never finished this side of the grave. For many, it continues beyond the grave in purgatory. However, there is no reason why we should wait until after death to complete the work of our sanctification. God desires that all of us should attain sanctity here upon earth before death. Each of us receives all the help we need to incarnate our nature into the supernatural life of grace. We must cooperate with these graces by strenuous efforts on our part. There is need of a great deal of patience with our faults, since sanctity is usually a long, drawn-out process. But if we persevere to the end, we shall be saved (Mt 24:13). This means a constant rising after each fall, never allowing discouragement to overwhelm us. It is to be expected that we will fall many times as we climb the mountain of perfection. Our heavenly Father is quick to forgive, provided we are willing to rise and keep climbing. Regardless of the past, God will give us the grace here and now to make a new start. Our best assurance for the future is to be generous with the Lord today.

This conversion of faults into virtues is called "metanoia" or penance. This was the message of Isaia to the chosen people of the Old Testament. This is likewise the message of Christ for the community of God's people under the New Covenant of love. This spirit of penance or metanoia has been the constant theme of Christian preachers throughout the centuries. The Good News of salvation can be accepted only by those who are willing to undergo a real conversion of their hearts toward good. Metanoia implies two things, a turning away from the evil toward which one's energies in the past have been directed; a positive turning of all our powers toward some good object. The legitimate objects for our love may be God, our brethren, ourselves and the world. But all these loves must be according to the proper order and balance that God wills for us. God must be the center and everything else must be oriented around him.

It is not easy to attain this balance, but the struggle will be the cross that brings salvation to us.

The first of the powers that needs to be converted is what St. Paul calls the "flesh." "The flesh lusts against the spirit and the spirit against the flesh" (Gal 5:17). In the original Greek, the word used for this evil tendency is "sarx." We might define "sarx" as everything in our nature that is hostile to God. It is unfortunate that we translate "sarx" as flesh, since this implies that our body is evil. Because of sin there exists in our nature tendencies to attribute evil to God. It is these hostile powers that lust against the Holy Spirit who also dwells within us through grace. Like the Hebrews in Egypt, all of us have been born into a condition of slavery to the "sarx." Original sin and the sins of our forefathers have implanted within us a hostility to God and we come into this world wearing this chain. Baptism does not completely free us from the "sarx," neither does the Sacrament of Penance. It is only by cooperating with the graces which the sacraments give us that we can gradually transform these hostile powers into energies of love. If the "sarx" ever conquers us, it will not be because God has failed to do his part, but because we have failed to correspond with his graces. We have real, external enemies who desire very much to lead us astray. However, we still remain masters of our own destiny, and can decide what we wish to do with our lives.

The aversion to God that dwells within each of us is encouraged by the hostile powers that are present in others. The more the other person has consented to evil, the worse will be his enmity toward us. When we are struggling manfully with our own "sarx," it is no help to come into the presence of someone who has long since made his decision against God. To encounter a really malicious person who deliberately hates God is a truly frightening experience. If we are still on the fence ourselves, unwilling to make a total commitment of love for God, this meeting with his enemy can easily be the final straw that causes us to reject God. On the other hand, if we have already thrown all our energies into the love of God, we may expect an open conflict with any enemies of God that we may meet.

If we can imagine the combination of hostility to God that dwells in all the people living in the world, we will understand what our Lord meant when he calls the world our enemy. "The world has hated them, because they are not of the world even as I am not of the world" (Jn 17:14). Just as we must make a distinction between our own flesh and our "sarx," so we must distinguish the world created by God from the combined "sarx" of the people in the world. It is this latter that is our enemy. Nevertheless, we must love this enemy, even while being on guard against it. Just as we have the task of converting our own "sarx" into love, so we must help the people of the world convert their evil tendencies into good. The best method of defense against the "sarx" is to struggle with it, striving to incarnate it into the Kingdom of God. Even if we do not succeed with others, the effort expended will protect us from being led astray and will help us complete the work of sanctification within ourselves.

Christ tells us that all hostility to God is centered in a definite person whom he calls "the prince of the world" (Jn 14:30). This enemy of God is Satan, once a beautiful angel who freely chose to become God's adversary. When Adam sinned, Satan and the other bad angels became the "world-rulers of this darkness" (Eph 6:12). At Baptism God "rescued us from the power of darkness and transferred us into the kingdom of his beloved Son" (Col 1:13). The power of Satan on earth will be destroyed forever when Christ comes the second time to complete the kingdom of the third aeon on earth. During this present "between-time," "Your adversary, the devil, as a roaring lion, goes about seeking someone to devour" (I Pt 5:8). "Woe to the earth and to the sea, because the devil has gone down to you in great wrath, knowing that he has but a short time" (Ap 12:12). As the prince of this world, Satan looks for allies among those worldly people who have given full vent to their "sarx." Through them God's adversary seeks to lead us away from the path of love. "In the last days dangerous times will come. Men will be lovers of self, covetous, haughty, proud, blasphemers, disobedient to parents, ungrateful, criminal, heartless, faithless, slanderers, incontinent, merciless, unkind, treacherous, stubborn, puffed up with pride, loving pleasure more than God; having a semblance of piety but disowning its power" (I Tim 3:1-5).

From the example of Christ in his Passion, we learn the power of love to turn the hatred of the world into an instrument of salvation. Through Christ's love, the greatest crime in history, the putting to death of the God-man, became the very act that saved us. If we follow the example of Christ, we can transform the hatred of our persecutors into a power for salvation, both for our enemies and many others, as well as ourselves. Our hearts must go out in love to those who are filled with hostility to God. Even if they cause us much suffering, we must continue to love them, pray for them and seek to help them transform their energies of hate into love. The more we ourselves have succeeded in sublimating our own "sarx" into love, the better able we will be to help our brethren. We have God's repeated promises in Sacred Scripture that good, not evil, will triumph in the end.

Final victory is assured, it awaits but the cooperation of men of good will. If we are willing to take up our cross and follow Christ, we will have a substantial share in the final fruits of the world's resurrection.

In God's original plan for mankind, there was no place for suffering. Pain and death entered the world as a result of sin: not merely as punishment but as a merciful means to rescue us from our "sarx." With the Passion and Death of Christ, a new dimension was added to our suffering—loving union with Jesus on the cross. It would be completely against nature and reason to consider suffering as the goal of our life. The death of Christ on Good Friday is the greatest manifestation of his love for us. "Greater love than this no one has, that one lay down his life for his friends" (Jn 15:13). The day of greatest triumph for Christ was his resurrection on Easter Sunday. Our day of triumph will be the new day of the third aeon when we also will rise victoriously from the grave.

XVI

Progress in Love

The life of grace and love must ever go forward during this second aeon. Since the time of St. Teresa of Avila, it has been customary to divide a soul's progress into seven mansions or stages. "God showed her a most beautiful crystal globe or diamond, made in the shape of a castle, containing seven mansions or courtyards. In the innermost of these mansions was the King of Glory in the greatest splendor and light, illuminating and beautifying all those souls living in each of the mansions. The nearer one got to the center, the stronger was the light. The differences in the intensity of the light, as one got farther from the center, resulted in seven distinct regions, marked by a series of concentric circles. Each of these seven mansions contained, in addition, many smaller circles or regions. Outside the castle all was foul, dark and infested with poisonous creatures" (Canonization process).

A person in mortal sin is entirely outside the seven mansions. Those in the first mansion are they who commit many deliberate venial sins and make many deliberate compromises in their service of God. Again and again they refuse knowingly to do what God expects of them, even though it be only in venial matters. It is comparatively easy for these souls to fall into mortal sin, and any who deliberately remain in this first mansion are greatly lacking in the love of God. They fear God's punishments and obtain forgiveness of their sins through imperfect contrition. The longer they remain in this first mansion, the more hardened they become to God's call of love. If this state is due to ignorance and lack of religious education, God will make allowances when he judges these souls. If, however, through sloth or some other fault one deliberately remains in it, there is grave danger of his regressing into a state of mortal sin and losing his soul.

Those in the second mansion are souls who no longer habitually commit deliberate venial sins. Nevertheless, they still make compromises with God through innumerable imperfections and venial sins which are partly deliberate. They lead rather mediocre lives, with many venial sins of passion, negligence and selfishness. They would never think of committing a mortal sin and get along reasonably well with everyone, including God. They are faithful to their religious duties, fulfilling at least the minimum requirements of prayer for their state of life. If laity, they probably go to confession and communion once a month, perhaps every Sunday to the Eucharist, if this is the custom of the place where they live. If religious, they are reasonably obedient to the rule and probably give little or no trouble to their superiors. If priests, they do a fairly good job of whatever work they are assigned. In general, those in the second mansion are the ordinary people in the Church who are content to fulfill their basic obligations towards God and neighbor. Their greatest danger is mediocrity. "I know thy works, thou art neither cold nor hot . . . because thou art lukewarm. . . . I am about to vomit thee out of my mouth" (Ap 3:16).

In their progress towards sanctity, nearly all souls go through a rather long struggle with mediocrity. If our souls follow the more or less average pattern, we will experience a period of religious or spiritual enthusiasm somewhere around the age of twenty. If we respond to God's call of love, there may be several years of fervor. Gradually the intensity of the love wears off and we usually find ourselves so occupied with other affairs that God and the life of grace are allowed to take a second place in our life. Externally, we may still remain faithful to the prayers and other spiritual exercises that we began some years previously. However, we no longer have the same enthusiasm for them. Progress through the second mansion can be compared to the long, hot desert journey from the Red Sea to the promised land. In our first conversion, we were able to free ourselves from the chains of sin that had been for us like the slavery of Egypt for the Hebrews. But a journey that begins with great enthusiasm can become quite discouraging as year after year passes without sight of the goal. Like the Jews in the desert, we may long to return to the flesh pots of Egypt.

To overcome the dangers of discouragement, it is essential that souls in the second mansion persevere in their desires for heroic sanctity and maturity. They must never be willing to settle for anything less than the best. They can keep their hopes high if they meditate frequently on the wonderful promises of God concerning the promised land of the third aeon. In one way or another, they must develop a resolute will, a firm step and a persevering effort in their struggle to keep going through the hot desert sands. In later mansions it will be possible to abandon oneself so completely into the hands of God that his grace will carry us along. In the early mansions, a constant effort is required on our part in order to cooperate with God's helping grace. Naturally, our main task is to strengthen our wills and develop great self-control. Supernaturally, our greatest effort is to keep alive the high hopes and tremendous desires for sanctity that are necessary to keep us going forward. Regardless of how many days in the past we have failed, each morning we must rise to a new day of struggle and dedicate ourselves to our work as though it were our first day.

God's helping grace will never be lacking to us as we struggle across the desert of the second mansion. From time to time we will experience some kind of a crisis, either natural or supernatural. One of these usually comes around the age of 28, another about the age of 35 when we enter the second half of our life on earth; a third crisis will develop about the age of 42. In addition to these major crises, there will probably be many others, small or great, depending upon the particular circumstances of one's life and God's special destiny for us. If we will correspond generously with God's call of grace in times of crisis, we will experience a new conversion or metanoia. We may not be aware of any substantial change in our life until sometime later, but for better or for worse, there will be a real turning point in our desert journey at these times. The decisions we make in times of crises are determined not merely by what we do then, but in a great measure they depend upon how faithfully we persevere in our efforts from day to day throughout the journey.

The passage from the second to the third mansion is usually one of the major crises in our life and is often called the second conversion. It is not necessarily a time of great suffering, but we should soon become aware of a major change in our attitude toward God and our neighbor. It may begin with a tremendous new enlightenment whereby we see ourselves as we really are in the light of God's truth. We realize that we have been struggling so long and yet still so far from our goal. Despite all our past efforts, the results we have to show are quite pitiful. At the rate we have been going, it is apparent that we will never succeed in reaching perfection, either natural or supernatural. This is the moment of real crisis with several possible choices facing us. We may decide to settle for a life of lukewarmness and mediocrity, willing to get by with a minimum of effort. On the other hand, we may choose to turn away completely from our goal either in despair or rebellion. Finally, we may decide to persevere in many heroic acts of blind faith and trust in God, plus a determination to cooperate with God's new calls of grace, regardless of the cost to ourselves. If our choice is the third one, we will gradually or even suddenly find ourselves looking at everything from a new standpoint. We will have entered a new relationship of love with God and with our brethren which is called the third mansion. The discouragements of the former mansion will be replaced with a tremendous conviction of God's goodness and God's personal love and care for each of us. "I am sure that neither death nor life, nor angels nor principalities, nor things present nor things to come, nor powers, nor height, nor depth, nor any other creature will be able to separate us from the love of God which is in Christ Jesus our Lord" (Rom 8:38-39).

A person in the third mansion is considered a very fervent Christian. Although still far from the heroic sanctity of the saints, life in this mansion does reach a certain level of perfection. Both naturally and supernaturally a high degree of maturity develops during the years spent on this level. From time to time, certain flashes of contemplation and direct experience of God's presence are given to these fervent souls as they progress toward the higher mansions. Ordinarily, there is still a long road to be traveled before the next mansion is attained; nevertheless the journey through the third mansion is usually much more pleasant than that of the earlier mansions.

One's life becomes a total dedication to the service of God and one's brethren. Fear is no longer an important factor in life; love, hope and joy are the predominant characteristics. Life is no longer centered in one's ego, but in loving and helping others to be happy. A great peace usually pervades one's whole person and all one's relationships with others. Those in this mansion experience many personal encounters of love with God during divine liturgy and at personal prayer and meditation. One learns to live constantly in the presence of God, thinking of him during every waking hour. The first thought upon awakening is that of God—gratitude for all that the Lord has given and offering of oneself to do his will during the day. A loving conversation is carried on with the Lord during every free moment. They are able to speak boldly and frankly to God, without any formalities or fears. Persons at this stage of sanctity will be very submissive to the least manifestation of God's will, without any resentment when God fails to do what is asked. Enough maturity and faith has been attained to realize that God always knows what is best and will do it, if one submits to his will.

Along with its many consolations, life in the third mansion has its crosses. Egocentricity is still strong so that one will experience temptations of pride, vanity, anger, discouragement, sensuality, resentment, selfishness. Besides the problems with one's own "sarx," the souls in this mansion frequently find themselves at odds with the "sarx" of others. Perhaps for the first time in their lives, they realize they have enemies, often among the very persons they had previously considered their friends. The dedicated life of a person in this mansion is a rebuke to those who have chosen mediocrity and compromise. People are disturbed by the extremes to which those in the third mansion go in their love and service of God and neighbor. The simplest way to counteract this disturbance is to criticize the actions of the fervent Christian. They seek some weak point in the character of the dedicated person, or if necessary, imagine something to be true which isn't. Frequently, other less fervent Christians are disturbed by the actions of one who, in their estimation, is an extremist. Persecution results and real suffering is inflicted upon the generous person. No real harm need come from this opposition; it can be used by the providence of God to purify the fervent soul of the remaining vestiges of pride and egocentricity. The persecution from one's brethren will prepare the man of fervor for the more difficult crosses of the dark nights which still lie ahead and need to be endured in order to reach the higher mansions. If one is faithful, after a period of suffering there will be a resurrection into a higher level of grace and wholeness.

XVII

Progress in The Natural Virtues

During the journey through the second and third mansions it is important that we emphasize the positive rather than the negative side of life. Both growth in virtue and the conquering of faults are necessary, but the greater attention should be given to the virtues. Since every fault is a misdirected virtue, any progress in the virtues will result in a corresponding weakening of our faults. Much effort needs to be given to the practice of both the natural and supernatural virtues. Since nature and grace normally should be balanced within us, we should aim at attaining a perfection of all the virtues needed for natural maturity as well as supernatural sanctity. None of the virtues can be strictly separated from the others; any progress in one will make easier the practice of all the others. Our goal in life is the incarnation of our whole nature into Christ, and a constant stream of helping grace is needed to accomplish this transformation. These will come to us through the liturgy and through prayer—our own prayers and the prayers of our friends. Without God and our brethren, it would be a hopeless task to attempt perfection. It is only by the cooperation of all, God, the community and ourselves, that the Kingdom of God will be reached.

Virtue of Honesty

Among all the natural virtues, the first and most important is that of honesty. It is the foundation of all maturity, both natural and supernatural. The absence of honesty in the Pharisees is what caused our Lord to condemn them so thoroughly. The lack of honesty in one's life will be the cause of countless physical, mental, emotional and spiritual troubles. In this sense, honesty is more important than goodness because any virtue that is built upon dishonesty will be a house built on sand or a house of cards, ready to collapse. God loves the honest sinner, the "publican," much more than he does the dishonest "saint"—the Pharisee. Honesty and natural humility are practically synonymous virtues. Honesty means the desire and the willingness to face the full truth about ourselves—to see ourselves as God sees us. We need to accept both our virtues as well as our vices; our fears, our weaknesses, our limitations, our failures, our loneliness—likewise, our blessings, our graces, our friends, everyone and everything that has helped us reach the stage of perfection we now enjoy. Not only are we willing to admit these things to ourselves, we are willing that others know them and we openly reveal them whenever the occasion demands it.

We are usually less good than what we imagine ourselves to be. It requires great effort and pain to face up to the many unpleasant facts about our character that are frequently seen by others but not by ourselves. It would be dangerous to our whole growth in perfection to be given a total revelation of our faults at one sitting. The first step is to face up to the probability that there is a vast number of evil tendencies in our unconscious that need to be brought to the surface, decontaminated and transformed into virtues. If we are humble, we will be able calmly to face the truth that we are capable of committing rather easily every sin that we have ever heard of in others. Knowing the truth about our own egocentricity, we will never despise our brethren, no matter how terrible they are. Realizing our own shameful practices of the past and the dangers of the present, our hearts will go out in understanding and love toward every sinner, even the worst.

In the process of attaining the perfection of honesty and humility, we will endure many crises. In the tension that results from our confrontation of our own dishonesty and evil, there is danger of a breakdown of our whole conscious life. Ordinarily, it is impossible to face alone the full truth about ourselves. We need at least one other person who also acknowledges the truth about us, yet still loves us and is willing to help us. The more evil we have committed in the past, the more necessary is this friend. Without his encouragement and love, there is grave danger of our falling victim to total discouragement and despair. It is the task of this friend, perhaps a spiritual director, to accept the full truth about ourselves without rejecting us but instead having high hopes for us. It is also his task to convince us that God still loves us even as we are and that with his grace it is not too late to achieve maturity and sanctity. Without a friend few, if any, of us, are able to face the full truth about ourselves and still survive. The faith and confidence that are needed to keep us progressing toward perfection, come not only from God but nearly always through our brethren.

Virtue of Courage

St. Thomas Aquinas defines courage as the virtue which strengthens us to do what reason dictates as right and to overcome the fear of danger and toil (I–II, q. 61, a. 2). Without courage we could never face the truth about ourselves and tackle the many difficult tasks needed to reach perfection. Both maturity and sanctity are fundamentally the proper exercise of love and the greatest enemy of love is fear. As long as our hearts are filled with excessive fear of God, of others, of the world, of ourselves, there will be no real progress in loving. Courage is the virtue that conquers fear; therefore, it is essential to any growth in natural and supernatural wholeness. With courage we are willing to experiment, to try new things, to take the chances necessary to go forward into the unknown. There is something new and fresh about every saint as well as every naturally mature person. Each of us must cut a new path through the jungle of life to the mountain of perfection. We can learn much from the experiences of our brethren in the past and the present, but there must never be slavish imitation. The life of each of us is a new day which holds out the exciting promise of things that have never been accomplished previously in the whole history of the world. Because it is new, it is also unknown, untrodden, untried. In every age of the world each person is meant to be a pioneer, boldly taking control of his destiny and venturing into new lands never previously conquered. In the beginning of a new age as our own, there is special need of a pioneering spirit among all Christians.

Where do we find the heroic courage needed to be a

saint and a pioneer? It will come first from God through the virtue of hope which is the supernatural incarnation of natural courage. Secondly, it will come from the courage and inspiration of our friends, either living or dead. It is a great help to read the lives of the saints and meditate on the tremendous courage they showed in trying new things, in overcoming fear and enduring suffering. Thirdly, it is possible to gain courage from the realization that the driving force behind all our fears and cowardice is actually the misdirected energy to love. If we will make the effort to direct this energy into the proper channels, we will soon overcome our fear of hard work, failure, disapproval, loneliness. With the help of God's grace, our friends and our own common sense we will find the wisdom needed for a courage that is daring but not fool-hardy.

Virtue of Prudence

Prudence is defined as the "right judgment of things to be done" (I–II, q. 57, a. 4). It is the common sense that enables us to make the right decisions about what to do. God insists that each of us assumes the responsibility for our life and actions. He will give us the grace to develop the prudence necessary for our particular vocation in life, but this grace does not work automatically. It requires exertion on our part to develop both the natural and supernatural talents we have been given. Through our study and experience with human nature and through the experiences of our brethren, we should grow in common sense as long as we live. It is possible to go to extremes on both sides of prudence. There are some who seem to be especially lacking in this virtue; while others are over-prudent, using it as an excuse for inactivity or cowardice. Through the Gift of

Counsel, the Holy Spirit gives us the grace to perfect the virtue of prudence. It is our responsibility to work hard to cooperate with the Holy Spirit in attaining the wisdom of good judgment.

Virtue of Art

St. Thomas says that art is the virtue that gives us the right judgment of the things to be made (I–II, q. 57, a. 3). All of us need to develop our talents of creativity, since every human being has the vocation of an artist, for an artist is one who possesses the ability to make things well. We are called to be co-creators with God in refashioning the things of creation until we have formed the renewed creation of the third aeon. The world, as we have it today, is the raw material out of which the Kingdom of God is to be made. God depends upon us to cooperate with him in creating this new heaven and new earth. Each of us has been given specific talents of creativity, and it is our task in life to develop these talents to their full capacity. Like any other virtue, art is capable of unlimited increase, provided we are willing to put forth the effort to educate ourselves. Besides God's helping grace, we must study under good artists who have developed their facility of making things well. Finally, our virtue of art needs the knowledge that comes from our own personal experience with many different materials and the continued exertion to make all things well.

The greatest of all arts is the direction of human beings toward maturity and sanctity. The raw material in this instance is the most precious of all God's creations—the human person with his spiritual soul and material body. All of us have the responsibility to be our brother's keeper and therefore, we are called in one way or another to work with people and to help them reach the perfection for which they are destined. Like all artists, we must have great reverence and respect for the material with which we work. We must not try to force others to do things for which they were not intended. We must have consideration for their freedom and avoid all dishonesty and artificiality. We must be very patient and willing to work long hours in helping them, without counting the cost or expecting any recompense. By studying the behavior of a really first-class artist, we can learn much of how we should act toward our brethren.

Virtue of Temperance

Every virtue is a balance between two extremes. Temperance is the virtue that curbs these extremes without destroying their power for good. It is like the harness and the bridle which make it possible for us to use the energies of a high-spirited horse without breaking his spirit. Through self-denial and self-control, one can make good use of his passions and powers without harm to anyone. All of our faculties, both spiritual and material, are gifts of God to be used in his service and in the service of our neighbor and ourselves. Because of sin, these powers have a tendency to usurp their proper position as servants to our will and thus become independent of all control. Much labor is needed to achieve moderation and balance among all these warring factions within our nature. It is particularly in the first twenty-five years of one's life that much self-denial should be practiced if we hope to use these great powers as our servants for good. Care must be taken not to kill them but to educate and control them. To weak and cowardly souls it often seems safer to destroy them, especially if they continue to give trouble. Nevertheless, it is in the very struggle to live under the tension of these extremes that we will find the strength to progress into the wholeness of maturity and sanctity. God's helping grace will not be lacking. If we cooperate with grace and have the example and guidance of good friends, we will in due time attain a proficiency with temperance. In the second half of our life, there should be enough good habits of self-control established so that we no longer need be afraid of our passions but can give our attention to the higher virtues, especially that of charity.

Virtue of Justice

Justice is giving to everyone what is due to him. Our Lord insists in the Beatitudes that every Christian should have an incessant hunger and thirst for justice. If we are to love God and our neighbor, the first duty of charity is to see that they receive all that is coming to them in justice. As long as injustice is present, no charity is possible. St. Thomas Aquinas puts all of man's religious duties under the virtue of justice, since they comprise the service that is due to God by the very nature of things. No one can consider himself a living Christian who is not vitally interested in bringing justice into all the areas of life where it is now lacking—race relations, international relations, undeveloped nations, the poor, downtrodden and persecuted people all over the world.

XVIII

The Gifts of the Holy Spirit

In our progress towards union with God, we need not only natural virtues; we have even greater need of the supernatural virtues of faith, hope and charity. Growth in these latter virtues is primarily the work of the Holy Spirit; but progress depends likewise upon our cooperation and the assistance of our brethren. The Gifts of the Holy Spirit are at work in every soul that is in the state of grace, but less noticeably and more silently for those in the early mansions. As one progresses toward heroic sanctity, the Seven Gifts of the Spirit become more and more evident. Another phenomenon about the Gifts is that they are especially observable in the community of God's people whenever there is a crisis that requires the special intervention of God. If the people cooperate with the Holy Spirit at these times, there will be a tremendous advance of the whole Church toward the completion of the Kingdom. Each gift of the Holy Spirit is a grace that we are free to accept or to refuse. Lest these Gifts be lost through ignorance, it is essential that we know all we can about the workings of the Spirit so that we can recognize them when offered and do our best to correspond with them.

Fear of the Lord

This gift is needed very specially by those in the first mansion of grace. Through it we realize the vast distance that separates God from us and thus appreciate what a terrible thing it is to flaunt oneself against the creator through disobedience to his will. This gift gives an understanding of the infinite transcendence of God above the world. When it is working in our souls, we show the proper reverence for God in prayer and otherwise. By means of natural knowledge we understand something of the omnipotence of God. The Holy Spirit takes this natural awesomeness and transforms it into the beautiful supernatural relationship of reverent love for all the things of God that we see in the saints. If we cooperate with the Gift of Fear of the Lord, our humility grows each day. Without discouragement we will be able to accept the truth of our nothingness, our absolute dependence upon God and all it means to be his creatures. With this respect for God in our hearts, temptations to pride and egocentricity are more easily conquered and the attractions of forbidden pleasures no longer allure us. All of our relationships with God, especially prayer, will be filled with the deep reverence which a creature owes to the Lord and Creator of all.

Piety

Piety balances Fear of the Lord by revealing to us that God is our heavenly Father as well as our Lord and Creator. By means of this gift we appreciate all it means to be a child of God. Even though we are vividly aware of the infinite greatness of our heavenly Father and our own nothingness, through the power of this gift we approach him on the most intimate terms of love. We realize that the primary relationship which God desires with us is not fear but the love of a father and a child. In our natural relationship with God, there must be balance between the awesome and the fascinating sides of God's nature. The Gifts of Fear of the Lord and Piety give a similar balance to our supernatural love and thus perfect nature. Love for all our brethren should increase as we realize that we are all children of the same heavenly Father. Our prayer life improves as Piety encourages us to speak most intimately and lovingly to each of the Persons of God. This gift is needed especially during the long desert journey of the second mansion. Convinced by the Holy Spirit of God's fatherly love and protection for us, we find the supernatural courage to progress more quickly across the dry, hot desert of this life towards the promised land of perfect love.

Knowledge

This gift enables us to see the things of this world as God sees them. This "new look" begins with the first infusion of sanctifying grace; however, it becomes particularly noticeable during the third mansion. At this period in life, so many former mysteries are made clear. One no longer keeps asking, "Why did God do this?" "Why did this have to happen to me?" By some kind of divine intuition, we begin to sense the reason for most of the things that happen. There will still be mysteries in God's dealings with mankind, but as one progresses in grace, these mysteries become less and less. At the moment of the event, one may not be able to see the loving hand of God's providence. However, if acts of faith and hope are made, rather quickly the Holy Spirit shows a soul in this mansion some good reasons why it was best. Through the gift of Knowledge, we more and more understand the truth of St. Paul's words, "For those who love God, all things work together unto good" (Rom 8:28).

All of life becomes filled with joy and enthusiasm for the future. One awakens each morning with delight that another day of God's grace has been given him. He arises with new energy from the Holy Spirit to tackle whatever problems it brings, knowing that the same God who has shown such wonderful care in the past, will be there to help today. Through the gift of Knowledge we are able to experience first-hand the providence of God. Seeing the things of earth in the light of divine truth, we lose our fears of God, of people, of the future, of ourselves. This gift perfects the virtue of faith by giving us a supernatural "extra sensory perception." Blindly but in reality nevertheless, we develop a certain intuition for the presence of God in each thing and event. Through Knowledge the Holy Spirit shows us the value of humiliations, failures, temptations, persecutions and sufferings of all kinds. Things which nature presents to us as evil, may appear as good by the light of this gift.

The gift of Knowledge enables us to put a proper order into our lives and the lives of those under us. It shows us the true value of each thing and its relationship to God and our goal of the Kingdom of God. At one time Knowledge gives us a distaste for creatures, when their attraction is a threat to our life of sanctity. At another time it will show us the wonderful beauties of God in nature and in creatures. All of our poetical and artistic abilities are enhanced through this gift, since it enables us to see the divine in everything of nature. Our practical judgments of the things of earth benefit through this supernatural gift of the Holy Spirit. Progress in natural maturity and wholeness is especially aided by the three gifts of Knowledge, Counsel and Fortitude.

Counsel

This is the gift that perfects the natural virtue of prudence and might be called its supernatural incarnation. It is a divine intuition that enables us to know God's will in our choice of words and actions. Through this gift, the Holy Spirit exerts a sweet compulsion upon our minds, giving us God's conscience of what is right and wrong in a given situation. It tells us when to speak or act, and when to be quiet and do nothing. Without any process of human reasoning, we are given a divine practical judgment for the particular matter at hand. Previously we may have been completely in the dark, but at the given moment for acting, we are shown the right word to say and the right action to take. An example of this gift was the decision of Pope John XXIII to have a Council of the Church. He tells us that without any previous thought about it, the words were suddenly on his lips while speaking to the Cardinals on January 25, 1959. Counsel becomes especially necessary in the fourth and higher mansions of grace, when a person, having set his own house in order, is able now to dedicate his whole life to others.

At times the gift of Counsel clouds our minds, so that we are left hesitant, confused and unable to act. If we are patient, accept the humiliation and remain full of confidence in God, some event of divine providence will occur to set us right. Through this gift we will be shown the right time for everything: "A time to plant and a time to uproot; a time to tear down and a time to build; a time to weep and a time to laugh; a time to mourn and a time to dance; a time to scatter stones and a time to gather them; a time to embrace and a time to be far from embraces; a time to seek and a time to lose; a time to keep and a time to cast away; a time to rend and a time to sew; a time to be silent and a time to speak; a time to love and a time to hate; a time of war and a time of peace" (Ecc 3:2-8). By means of counsel, the Holy Spirit will show us how to be both firm and gentle; merciful and just; considerate and strict; truthful yet prudent. We will know how to keep secrets and still speak without telling a lie.

Fortitude

It is not enough to know what to do, we need the courage to act upon the light which the Holy Spirit gives us. The Gift of Fortitude is the supernatural incarnation of natural courage and the perfection of the virtue of Christian hope. Natural courage alone is not enough to enable us to cooperate with supernatural Knowledge and Counsel. The gift of Fortitude is needed in times of crisis when courageous decisions must be made. Often it is only by the help of the Holy Spirit that we find the strength to leave our old, accustomed ways and to rise to a higher level of maturity and sanctity. Fortitude is needed most of all when a soul is suffering the dark nights of struggle that must be endured in order to reach the heights of heroic charity. Without the special help of the Holy Spirit no soul can arrive in the higher mansions of passive contemplation. By this gift of Fortitude we are given the courage of God himself to overcome the difficulties that naturally would be impossible to conquer. Counsel and Knowledge bring reason to perfection, while Fortiude perfects the will and the passions. In this gift we receive the grace to suffer with Christ whatever agony it is God's will to permit us. At times we are left weak and prostrate like Christ in Gethsemane; but at the right moment supernatural strength is given so that we can, like the martyrs, endure the greatest possible suffering with joy and peace, provided we cooperate. All the mansions of grace need and possess Fortitude, but it becomes especially notice-able in the three highest mansions.

Understanding

The gift of Knowledge concerns the things of creation, while Understanding enlightens us in the supernatural mysteries of our Christian faith. Souls in the higher mansions are especially gifted with this grace of Understanding. Through this gift we are given new insights into Sacred Scripture and the teachings of the Church, seeing things that in the past we never suspected. Understanding enables us to penetrate the veils of faith and opens to us many new dimensions of revealed truth in the Bible. Without any dependence upon earthly images, the Spirit fills the mind with an intuitive knowledge of the divine life shared by the Father, Son and Holy Spirit. This blinding, supernatural light of the Holy Spirit may leave the soul still wrapped in mystery, unable to find words to express what was revealed. "He was caught up into paradise and heard secret words that man may not repeat" (2 Cor 12:4). Through the gift of Understanding one is given unshakable convictions about the reality of God and the mysteries of our faith. Although still living in the darkness of the second aeon, a soul filled with Understand-ing will possess great joy and peace in the possession of God's truth. "Oh the depth of the riches, of the wisdom and of the knowledge of God" (Rom 11:33).

Wisdom

The greatest of all the gifts is Wisdom—the perfection of the virtue of charity. It enables a soul to find joy only in loving God and is a foretaste of the joys of heaven and the third aeon. Wisdom gives a soul a supernatural relish and delight for God and all the things of God. "Taste and see how good the Lord is" (Ps 33:9). Having tasted the joys of the Lord, one can no longer find satisfaction in the things of the earth apart from God. One now feels completely at home with the Lord and the only happiness is to possess God's love more and more. Wisdom enables a soul to embrace with sincere delight everything of God's will and to find peace and joy in the very midst of suffering, humiliation, persecution and death. By this gift the final sanctification of the soul is completed and one is ready to enter immediately into God's presence at the moment of death. Although present somewhat in all the mansions, it is possessed fully in the spiritual marriage of the seventh and highest mansion of grace. Through the outpouring of Wisdom the whole community of God's people are now able to progress more swiftly toward their final fulfillment in the Kingdom of the Last Day.

XIX

The Fruits of the Holy Spirit

Our Lord tells us in the Sermon on the Mount, "by their fruits you shall know them" (Mt 7:16). The working of the gifts of the Holy Spirit is often unconscious and unknown even to ourselves. This is especially true of the higher gifts of the Spirit—Wisdom, Understanding, Counsel and Fortitude. Usually they work in such beautiful cooperation with our natural powers that it is often impossible to distinguish between nature and grace. However, if we put no serious obstacles to the activity of the seven gifts of the Holy Spirit, it will not be long before the fruits of the Spirit will be evident to ourselves and to those with whom we live. The more we progress in the life of grace, the more manifest will be these fruits. St. Paul names eleven of them: "The fruit of the Spirit is—charity, joy, peace, patience, kindness, goodness, faithfulness, gentleness, moderation, self-control, purity" (Gal 5:22-23—*Missel Biblique*).

Everyone living in grace should enjoy something of each of these blessings of the Holy Spirit. During the first three mansions of grace, one may expect only an occasional experience of the fruits. With one's entrance into the fourth and higher mansions, the results of the work of the Spirit within our being become more open and constant. In the saint who has already attained the highest mansion of spiritual marriage with the Holy Trinity, the enjoyment of all the fruits should be very great and continuous. In this sense he will have already begun his heaven on earth, since life in the kingdom of God after death will simply be an ever deepening and everlasting possession of the wonderful fruits of the Spirit. Therefore, any valid growth in one or the other of these fruits is definite proof that we are on the right road toward the supernatural maturity called sanctity. We have here eleven tests by which we can determine whether we are being led by the good Spirit or by some other spirit that is opposed to God.

Charity

The first of these tests is called charity and it will ever be the most distinguishing mark of a true follower of Jesus Christ. Charity is a very special Christian virtue which goes exceedingly deeper than any purely natural love. To possess charity is to love others, both God and man, as Jesus Christ loves us. The whole New Testament is filled with the explanation and examples of this greatest of the fruits of the grace-life. If we are growing daily in grace, it should be apparent both to ourselves and to others that our charity is constantly increasing. In the earlier mansions, we may be able to see this growth only from year to year. As we progress into the higher mansions, the rate of increase in charity should become faster and faster. There will be periods when each day we experience an ever widening and deepening of this wonderful fruit of charity. At other times, the increase will be taking place deep in our psyche without any observable growth on the surface of our conscious life. However, in due time this unconscious evolution will suddenly break out into new and tremendous deeds of charity which will surprise even ourselves. Anyone who does not experience a more or less constant expansion of his charity toward God and his fellow-man should be concerned about the state of his supernatural growth.

The increase of charity can be compared to the stages of development in a natural relationship of love between a man and woman. First, there is a period of getting acquainted when they gradually become more and more fascinated with all that they learn about each other. The next period is that most delightful experience of falling in love. Not only does one enjoy the beloved, but the whole world is seen in a new light—the light of this newly found love. The third period is called courtship, followed by an engagement or solemn and permanent promise of everlasting love. The climax of this natural relationship of love is found in the espousals of a marriage that will unite them forever.

God created these beautiful blessings of natural love, sex and marriage, in order to help us better understand the meaning of that fruit of the Holy Spirit called Christian charity. What happens on a natural level when a man and woman love each other also takes place as each person advances through the mansions of the supernatural realm of grace. By means of the gifts of Knowledge, Piety and Fear of the Lord, we become supernaturally fascinated with God and with Jesus Christ dwelling within our brethren. This occurs during the first three mansions of our grace-life when we are getting to know and become attracted toward God, our neighbor and the things of God. In the fourth mansion we literally fall in love with God and all our brethren who are made to the image and likeness of God. Anyone who reaches the fourth mansion will never have any problem with loving those of a different race or background, since through the power of the Holy Spirit he sees God in them and becomes "head over heels" in love with them. This supernatural experience of "falling in love" with God and our brethren is exceedingly more delightful and satisfying than even the greatest natural relationship of love. The Gifts of the Holy Spirit, especially that of Wisdom, enables us at this time to see everyone and everything in a new light—the light of God himself. Seeing God everywhere, we feel a sweet but tremendous compulsion to love and serve him as he has never been loved and served in the past.

Having arrived this far in the progress of our charity, we are ready for a "whirlwind" courtship with God and all those who belong to God in any way—in other words, with all creation. We call this the fifth mansion of grace. Courtships are usually difficult since they require the necessary adjustment of our personality to the temperament and disposition of the beloved. However, if true love is present in both persons, they will help each other overcome the obstacles which separate them from the permanent union of marriage. At this fifth stage of the development of our grace-life, the Holy Spirit comes to our help by means of the Gifts of Counsel and Fortitude. We are not only enlightened by the Spirit as to the requirements of charity toward God and neighbor, but we are strengthened through the grace of Fortitude to carry out our obligations of supernatural love. Sacrifice on our part will be necessary in every mansion of grace, if we ever hope to attain the perfection of charity. However, it is in the fifth mansion that most souls can expect to experience their darkest nights of suffering. Until now, they didn't really know what they were missing when they were lacking the love of God and neighbor; but having fallen so deeply in love with God during the fourth mansion, they now experience something of the loneliness of hell itself whenever God seems to withdraw from them. If this experience of withdrawal by God is due to their own fault, it is not difficult to imagine how intensely a person would suffer at this time. Actually, the main reason for God's apparent withdrawals is to purify and increase our love for him. Even though one's faith and trust in God may tell him that this is true, nevertheless, any separation from the God whom we now love so deeply is a real agony of body and soul.

The courtship between God and a human being continues throughout the fifth mansion and it may be compared to a whirlwind. Light and darkness, joy and suffering often succeed one another quickly and suddenly. First we are picked up by God and find ourselves soaring into the "third heaven" mentioned by St. Paul (2 Cor 12:2). Then, without warning, we seem to be dropped into depths of darkness that are far removed from God. Not every person on the way to the seventh mansion is required to experience the dark nights of the soul described by St. John of the Cross. Just as there is an unlimited variety of experiences in natural courtship, the same can be expected in its supernatural counterpart of the fifth mansion. No two souls are ever treated by God in the same way. He seems to take great delight in using an infinite variety of methods in leading us to the heights of supernatural maturity. Regardless of the natural situation in which we find ourselves, the long arm of God's love is able to reach out to us, to rescue us and lead us by means of some new and strange path to the very top of the mountain of perfection. What a consolation it is for us to realize that no condition in life is hopeless when brought face to face with God's infinite love for us. Ideally we might expect the saint to have attained both natural and supernatural maturity. Actually, there are many canonized saints who were naturally immature and neurotic during the whole of their life on earth. God simply asks each of us to do what we can ourselves, then pray and depend on God's love to fill in the missing gaps. Ultimately, our salvation and sanctification always depend upon God's loving mercy. It is especially during the fifth mansion of grace-life that we vividly experience our own utter helplessness and God's unlimited mercy and love. "For it is God who of his good pleasure works in you both the will and the performance" (Phil 2:13).

As soon as God is satisfied with the depth and extent of our charity for him and his whole creation, the great moment has arrived for us to enter into a solemn commitment of our love for God and God's love for us. The period of this supernatural engagement is called the sixth mansion of grace. Comparing it to an engagement between a man and woman before marriage, this next to the last mansion is a busy time of preparation for the never-ending union with God which is called spiritual marriage. Through the Gift of Understanding, the Holy Spirit reveals to us what our divine spouse desires of us. Because he is such a tremendous lover himself, God's demands of love are exceedingly great. In all truth we must learn to love others as Jesus Christ loves us. Therefore, we must again and again study the life of Christ in the Gospels as well as the Epistles of St. Paul and St. John to learn what is expected of a spouse of God. Not only must we learn to love as God loves, but we must actually begin to love God and others as he loves us. If we have been faithful to God's grace throughout the previous mansions, we will have already attained a truly heroic degree of this fruit of charity. Now will be the time to polish off the rough edges to complete our preparations for the great day of our supernatural espousal with God.

Unfortunately, it would seem that few persons on earth

ever attain the seventh mansion before death. Many experienced authorities on the life of grace maintain that God gives to everyone sufficient grace to attain this seventh mansion of sanctity before death. It is still a mystery why more of us do not experience on earth the spiritual marriage with God for which we have been destined. We can at least be grateful for the purification of purgatory which will complete the unfinished business of our present life. Nevertheless, God would prefer that we should have our purgatory on earth. If we truly love God, we will try to cooperate perfectly with all of God's graces so that when we die we will be ready instantly to enter into the beatific vision of heaven. This is what God wants and this should be what we desire with all the intensity of our being. Unless we desire perfection to the degree that we are willing to pay any price to attain it, the chances are that we will die in the second or third mansion. This will mean that we will have to wait until after death for the purification that ordinarily should have been accomplished during the fourth, fifth, sixth and seventh mansions on earth.

Since God treats every person in a different way, it is impossible to give any exact schedule of the years that one needs to spend in the different mansions. It is likewise extremely difficult for anyone but the most experienced spiritual director to determine what is the exact mansion of grace in which a person is now living. One reason for this is that each of us is like a piece of cork bobbing up and down on a stormy sea. Ordinarily, we do not stay entirely in one mansion, but in the period of a year we might pass up and down the scale of several mansions. There may be moments when a soul in one of the earlier mansions is given a real foretaste of the life of union with God which is constantly enjoyed by those in the seventh mansion. Usually at the time of ordination, religious profession or other great moments of grace, the Holy Spirit lifts up one's soul into some higher mansion of grace. This experience of union with God may continue for some time before one finds himself back in his old habitat. If we cooperate as best we can with God's graces at these times of special fervor, life will never be the same as a result of these new experiences. Nevertheless, it is always possible to regress and lose the particular mansion in which we have been living for a long time. In the average person, there are many such regressions. Because God's merciful love for each of us is so great, it is always possible to recoup the losses we have suffered, provided we are still alive and in possession of our faculties. Therefore, regardless of what our situation has been in the past, there is never any reason for discouragement. As long as there is life, there is hope. "Whoever perseveres to the end, he shall be saved" (Mt 24:13).

To encourage those who are older and still find themselves struggling in one of the earlier mansions, it is a great consolation to know that the rate of progress in the life of grace increases its speed in a way similar to that of a falling stone. In the higher mansions, one is able to accomplish more in one month than could have been done in ten years earlier in life. Then, too, we must never shorten the arm of God's merciful love. If he so wills, he can accomplish at the moment of death or at some other moment in life what would ordinarily take a lifetime to attain, presuming the ordinary graces of God. This is why we must never give up our hope and desire to become a saint, no matter how old we are or how many years we have wasted in the useless pursuit of worldly pleasures. It is never too late, provided we throw ourselves completely into the arms of God's loving mercy. He loves us so much that he is willing to take us back, no matter how long or how much we have sinned against him. He will always be a true father, a true friend and a true spouse to us, regardless of how often we have failed him. "Who shall separate us from the love of Christ? Shall tribulation or distress or persecution or hunger or nakedness or danger or the sword. . . . In all these things we overcome because of him who has loved us" (Rom 8:35-37). It is evident that St. Paul had many experiences of the fruit of charity.

Joy

The second fruit of the Holy Spirit mentioned by St. Paul is joy. Our whole life of grace is meant to be a joyful experience. As St. Teresa of Avila put it, "All the way to heaven is heaven too." This does not mean that we can expect a life of smooth sailing into higher and higher attainments of pure joy. If we placed absolutely no obstacles to the working of grace in our soul, this indeed would happen. Due to our weakness and our failures, the way to perfect joy has many ups and downs. Nevertheless, as one progresses through the different mansions, one will become more and more aware of a constantly increasing joy of the spirit. As we grow in grace we should gradually find more joy in the possession of God and the things of God. One of the areas where this joy should especially be experienced is in our prayer-life. In the first mansions, prayer is usually difficult. We don't feel at home with God and find no great consolation in being alone with him. Ordinarily God will encourage souls in these earlier mansions with occasional experiences of consolation. However, after a time these first joys are usually removed and one's faith and trust in God is then tested by dryness and distractions in time of prayer. If one perseveres, he will at last come to taste the joys of what the theologians call passive contemplation. A foretaste of this wonderful fruit of the Holy Spirit will be experienced from time to time during the first three mansions of grace-life. It is in the fourth mansion that a soul begins more or less permanently to experience the tremendous joy of uninterrupted contemplation of God. From then to the seventh mansion, one thinks of God every moment of the day and night. Frequently this dwelling upon God is so deep and simple that the person involved is not aware of it. Nevertheless, the result will be a certain joy of the spirit that is apparent to others, if not to oneself. This inner joy will be present even in the midst of the darkest nights of suffering that the soul might be enduring. The proof of the presence of this joy is the fact that regardless of the situation or the price to be paid, a person in the higher mansions would never want to part from God. Even while suffering grave temptations and assaults from the evil spirits, the possession of the thought of God is so precious that one refuses to stop thinking about him.

Pleasure is a very superficial and passing phenomenon that is entirely different from this fruit of the Holy Spirit called joy. Pleasure and suffering are contradictory, but this is not true of suffering and joy. In the higher mansions, not only do they alternate with one another in taking possession of the spirit of a person, but they are frequently present at one and the same time. This is one of those Christian paradoxes that we see present so often in the lives of the saints. In the midst of the greatest possible persecution and suffering, the martyrs, for example, experienced the most intense joy. In the Canticle of the three Hebrews in the fiery furnace we celebrate one such experience of joy in suffering. Because all this is so contrary to the normal experience of nature, the fruit of joy is one of the best of all signs of the presence of the Holy Spirit within our souls. Anyone can be happy when all is going well with him; it is only those living in the higher mansions that are able to possess their souls in sincere joy even in the midst of pain, persecution and temptation. Those who have been given this fruit of joy should be ever grateful to the Holy Spirit.

Peace

St. Thomas Aquinas defines peace as the tranquillity of order. From the words of our Lord to the apostles at the resurrection we know that peace is one of the fruits of the Holy Spirit. "Peace be to you. . . . Receive the Holy Spirit" (Jn 19:21-22). Christ came to reestablish peace and order between God and man, heaven and earth. Every sin is a disorder of the relationship that should exist between ourselves and God or with our brethren. It is the work of the Holy Spirit to restore the tranquility of the beautiful and orderly relationship of love that originally existed in paradise. This will be accomplished through the forgiveness of sins and the progress of love, both naturally and supernaturally. If we abandon ourselves completely to the working of the Holy Spirit, we will gradually experience an ever greater peace. This fruit of the Spirit must be purchased at the high price of sacrificing our will to the will of God. The real disorder in the world that destroys peace is found in the human will. At first sight, one imagines that he will find peace and satisfaction in doing his own will. Actually, the very opposite is true. The more we progress in the mansions of grace, the more we will experience this truth.

Even those in the first mansions are able to enjoy something of this fruit of peace. The joy of a good conscience leaves our soul very much at peace. With tranquillity we are able to face the problems of life as long as we know that everything is in its proper order. Even in the midst of the greatest sufferings and temptations, it is possible for a soul to find himself at peace with himself, with God and with his neighbor. As one progresses through the higher mansions, this possession of peace becomes more evident, both to ourselves and to those with whom we live. The example of our peace of soul becomes a great inspiration to those around us. It is so evident that there is no natural explanation for the peace we have, perhaps in the midst of great opposition or persecution. If it is a sincere peace, it will persist regardless of the external circumstances of our life.

Patience

A fruit of the Holy Spirit closely allied to peace is patience. How delightful it is to ourselves and to all those with whom we live if we have been given this wonderful grace of patience—patience with others, patience with ourselves and patience with God. There can be a natural patience that is due either to one's disposition or to the strenuous efforts made to overcome anger. However, this particular fruit of the Spirit is a supernatural gift entirely beyond natural patience. It will be experienced at times and places where there can be no natural explanation for its existence. It will be quite evident, even to the person experiencing this fruit, that this is something entirely beyond his own efforts. It is simply a gift of the Spirit that enables him to rise above the natural situation and meet it with the patience of God himself. Those who possess this fruit will know how to wait patiently upon the movements of God's grace. Despite their intense desires to grow in love and sanctity, they will be patient with the Lord when he sees fit to delay his coming for many years. This same patience will be shown with themselves, their faults and imperfections. They will strive manfully to grow daily in perfection, yet be willing to keep working despite the many years they have had to stay in the second or third mansion. Even though they may find themselves in middle-age or even older without having arrived at the higher mansions, their faith and hope in God will be such that they continue to possess their souls in patience. Finally, their relationships with others will more and more be governed by an unlimited patience with the faults and failures of those around them. Despite every appearance to the contrary, they will continue to hope for the best and to help everyone who comes to them. This fruit of patience is one that can be more easily measured than some of the other fruits. For this reason, it is especially valuable as a test to determine whether we are progressing in the life of grace.

Kindness

This is another fruit that can be easily observed both in ourselves and in others. If we are growing in grace, our sincere kindness toward others should become more and more apparent. Without any natural explanation, we will find ourselves able to be kind to those whom naturally we might be expected to dislike. It is evident that the Holy Spirit is working within the depths of our soul and entirely beyond our natural capability. How fortunate we are when we have the privilege to live with a person who has attained one of the higher mansions. We can be sure of their great kindness toward us, regardless of what we do or how we might fail them. Their possession of this fruit of the Spirit enables us to have a tremendous confidence and security in their presence. Through their inspiration, we ourselves find the courage to return to the struggle needed to attain the heights of grace they have already received.

Goodness

It is nice that St. Paul placed goodness as one of the fruits of the Spirit. It sums up all those qualities which he did not have the time to place in his list of fruits. Anyone living and progressing in the life of grace should manifest a more or less constant goodness to all those around him. He will be one who shows himself more and more selfless in his efforts to be good to others. As he develops from one mansion to the next, this generosity in giving himself will become more evident. Those who live with him will know for sure that the Holy Spirit is showing his good pleasure by constantly increasing this fruit of goodness within his person and in all his actions.

Faithfulness

When we look for a friend, we want someone whom we can trust, one who is completely faithful. For this reason we should try to choose our friends among those who have reached the higher mansions, since the Holy Spirit enables these persons to perfect their natural dispositions of trustworthiness as well as enjoy the fruit of a supernatural fidelity. As one grows in grace-life, people will come more and more to depend upon him, knowing that he can always be trusted. They soon learn that he is always faithful to his word, his commitments and his loved ones. He can always be counted upon to do the right thing when handling a situation. This faithfulness will be seen not only in his devotion to the welfare of others, it will also be present in his fidelity to his duties to God, to all the duties of his state of life. In order to know for sure that the manifestation of faithfulness is a true fruit of the Spirit, one needs to compare his present life with the situation as it existed previously. If there is evidence of sudden increases in one's fidelity for which there is no natural explanation, the presumption is that the Holy Spirit is at work within the depths of the soul.

Gentleness

As a person grows in grace, a wonderful balance results in all the diverse sides of his character. It is usually difficult to determine the natural temperament of those in the higher mansions because the Holy Spirit has compensated for those things that were lacking in nature. An example of this is the fruit of gentleness that begins to appear in the life of a person who earlier in life may have been quite severe. Through the power of the Holy Spirit, all the best qualities of both masculinity and femininity will be present in those now living in the higher mansions. It is especially beautiful when someone who is eminently masculine is found to be filled with a deep tenderness and gentleness toward all those in need. It is so far beyond the natural expectations that we have good evidence of the presence of the Holy Spirit.

Moderation

Ordinarily, virtue stands in the middle between two extremes. From a natural point of view the virtue of prudence is given to help us strike the right balance in each situation of life. Nevertheless, there will be many times when natural pru-

dence is not sufficient to cope with the difficulties that arise. In these cases, the gift of Counsel is given a soul living in grace to enable him to make the right decision. The fruit of moderation will be the happy result of this supernatural grace of Counsel. St. Augustine, in his Confessions, makes the observation that it is more difficult to use something in moderation than it is to sacrifice it completely. It is certainly not God's will for us to deny all the goods and pleasures of this life; hence the need of this fruit of moderation, which will become more and more evident in the higher mansions. The proof that this is the fruit of the Holy Spirit will be found in the comparison of one's life now with the way it was at some earlier period.

Self-Control

During the first three mansions of grace, a hard and painful effort is required to bring one's nature under control. In the higher mansions this self-control becomes such a part of the person, that it seems to be completely natural. However, one needs only to think back to the struggle that was required to attain this control of self in earlier life, and it will be clear that something supernatural is definitely at work. In the first mansions, almost everyone has problems with the control of his passions, especially that of sex. Through the gifts of the Holy Spirit, these passions will be sublimated and incarnated into the life of grace. These energies will not be neurotically repressed but, through the power of the Spirit, will be siphoned into an energy for a pure, selfless love of God and man. In the original state of mankind, all his natural energies were at the service of his will, which in turn was completely obedient to God. By means of the gifts of the Spirit, something of the original self-control is restored to a human being.

Purity

For most people purity is considered a negative virtue with particular reference to chastity. Teilhard de Chardin defines purity as the power and goodness which is in our lives when the love of God is sought everywhere and above everything. Our purity is measured by the degree of attraction that draws us toward the divine center present in every person and every thing. Anyone possessing the fruit of purity will be able to see only God and the things of God when he looks at another person or thing. He will be greatly attracted by this goodness of God in others and will desire to draw as close as he can to it. Possessing a singleness of vision, he will seek to be united by the closest bonds of pure love to the goodness of God which is shared by the other.

Before arriving at such an exalted purity, a long process of purification is required. Traditionally this has been called the Purgative Way and it may be applied not only to the more active purification of the first mansions, but likewise to the passive purification that God accomplishes throughout one's journey toward supernatural maturity. Besides purification there is needed a constant growth in the light of God's grace. From ancient times this has been named the Illuminative Way. This also is subject to a continuous increase throughout the seven mansions. Both the negative purgation of evil and the positive illumination of grace exist for the sole purpose of leading us to the union of love between God and our whole being. This Unitive Way actually begins with the first entrance of a soul into the life of sanctifying grace. However, it reaches its fulfillment only in the seventh mansion of spiritual, supernatural marriage. It is here that the fruit of purity is experienced in all its fullness— without losing one's own personal identity, one becomes united to God in an everlasting marriage.

As one grows in grace, there will be less and less divergence and more and more unity. It will be discovered that there is but one word to describe this unity which we see in God, in the universe, in ourselves, between ourselves and others. It is the word—"love." And now we understand why we attribute all these wonderful fruits to the Holy Spirit: because the Holy Spirit is the Spirit of Love which unites the Father and the Son and, likewise, unites us to God through grace. "That the love with which thou hast loved me may be in them, and I in them" (Jn 17:26).

XX

Our Vocation in the Communion of Saints

There is an infinite variety to the possibilities of our experiencing the Gifts and Fruits of the Holy Spirit. All those who, in one way or another, are united to the Holy Spirit, form a community of persons which is called the Communion of Saints. Whether these persons be in heaven, purgatory or on earth, they are bound by the closest of all ties—that of the Spirit of God. Just as the Holy Spirit of Love joins the Father and Son in the Blessed Trinity, this same Spirit unites the great brotherhood of Christians throughout the earth to the souls of the just in heaven and purgatory. The fellowship which we enjoy in the Communion of Saints is a two-way street. Through the Holy Spirit, we are able to help others and they, in turn, can help us. The more traffic there is between the different members of the family of God, the more quickly we will reach our consummation on the Last Day. The coming of God's Kingdom and the personal salvation of each member is the concern of all the other members. In the world of grace there is no place for rugged individualism or selfishness. What we have received so generously from God through the Church, we must endeavor to share with our brethren. Gratitude to God and love for our fellow-travelers urge us to do everything possible to give others the wonderful graces that have been given us.

Our work for souls should be intimately connected with the particular vocation we choose. Our apostolic endeavors were never meant to be a mere sideline, while our main effort was directed to pleasing ourselves and the world. Instead, we should study our talents and abilities and determine how we can best use them to further the Kingdom of God upon earth. There are many tasks that need to be performed in order to bring to completion the Communion of Saints. We need the institution of Marriage to generate the love and the people who will complete the number of the elect. We need to eat, sleep, travel, be clothed, warmed and protected, as well as baptized, confirmed, forgiven and nourished with the Sacraments. God has generously bestowed upon mankind a variety of gifts and interests, so that all the needs of the human family will be fulfilled. It is the duty of each of us to find the particular way that we can best help our brethren. Whenever we discover our proper vocation, we will find a deep satisfaction in doing well the things for which we were created.

It is not easy to determine the particular work we should do in life. To add to the difficulties, we live in an age where the majority of people have distorted ideas about the purpose of work. How many people realize that its primary purpose is to serve God and our fellow-man? We do not merely work in order to live, but rather we should live so that we can work and help others to attain the fullness of life, both natural and supernatural. Work is not a curse imposed by God upon mankind; it is only the burden of sweat and toil that was added to the original command to "till and keep" the garden (Gn 2:15). Instead of trying to escape work by finding the job with the most pay and the least effort, our attitude should be that of Christ and the heavenly Father: "My Father works even until now and I work" (Jn 5:17).

If we are normal and healthy and if we have found the tasks for which we are best suited, all of us should find great joy and satisfaction in our work.

When our educators properly fulfill their assigned tasks, the average person is ready to choose his vocation at the beginning of adulthood. The young adult should consult older and wiser persons before deciding upon his life's work. The Holy Spirit should also be consulted through prayer and meditation upon the Kingdom of God and its needs. Then, after proper deliberation, a choice should be made and preparation should begin for it. Ordinarily, there should be no looking back or continued searching for greener fields. If a mistake has been made, divine providence will indicate clearly what he should do. Presuming that he has made a sincere effort to discover God's will, it is essential for his peace of mind that he believe the Lord will not abandon him. Even if we make a mistake, the Lord is able to arrange things, so that there will be abundant opportunity to do our part in completing the Kingdom of God. "For those who love God, all things work together unto good" (Rom 8:28).

As far as possible, we should live in the present, without too much concern about the past or the future. We should take each day as it is given us and with the time and energy available, do everything possible to be of service to God and our brethren. For most of us, there will always be more tasks to do than we have the time or ability. We should try to choose the more important; do them well and let the others go undone. We will eventually discover that these other tasks were either not important or that someone else did them. In our choice of the work to be done, we must observe the proper order of love. Those with the greatest need merit our first attention; and if there are several with the same need, we choose the one who has the first right to our love.

We will often make mistakes in judgment, but this is not important, provided we are sincere and generous in what we do. We must give and give and give, without counting the cost. Having received so much, it is now our vocation to share these good things with others. We should not demand that they appreciate what we are doing for them, since our purpose is to show appreciation for what God and others have already given us. Realizing that we have but a few years to spend upon earth, we should be determined to do as much good as we can with the resources available. We take up where our brethren of a former generation had to stop; we simply carry on the work of creation and salvation another step. When we die, we can hope that God will provide others to carry his Kingdom a further step toward completion. The burden of the whole world does not depend upon any one of us. Each of us is needed for the particular contribution that divine destiny has planned for us. Some are asked to give more than others, but we should all be as generous as we possibly can. Like Christ, we must spend our time, "going about doing good" (Acts 10:38). "I must do the works of him who sent me while it is day; night is coming when no one can work" (Jn 9:4).

In our efforts to help others, we must learn to work as a team with our brethren and not try to do our job alone. First of all, we need the advice of those wiser and more experienced than ourselves. We need friends and perhaps the greatest of all our friends will be the spiritual director, who guides us in making the decisions needed to attain maturity and sanctity. God has shared his gifts with many people and there is so much to be done that we must find a place for every person who is willing to work. Not only must we give help to others, we must allow them to aid us in our needs. It is not charity for us always to be giving and never receiving; very often the greatest favor we can do for a person is to give him the opportunity to be useful and to make a worthwhile contribution to our own happiness as well as to the happiness of others.

God had very good reason for creating us weak and in need of help from each other. This serves to keep us humble and encourages our friends to exercise their charity toward us. Realizing our great needs, we should turn without hesitation to the other members of the Communion of Saints and beg humbly for their help. Our salvation often depends upon these brethren of ours. Only after death shall we realize how much we owe to the prayers of the saints and angels in heaven and the souls in purgatory. As to the help we receive from the Communion of Saints on earth, all of us realize how greatly dependent is our salvation upon our parents, teachers, directors, superiors and other spiritual friends. If God had so chosen, he could have created some other dispensation of grace in which we would have received our salvation directly from the Lord. There are some people who, in proud independence, would like to think that this is still the way to be saved. Despite what they may think, it is through the Community of God's people that we receive the necessary grace.

At the head of the Communion of Saints is Jesus Christ, the God-Man. He is the mediator of the new covenant of love under which all of us have been born and will be saved. Instead of standing alone, Christ has willed to include our efforts and sacrifices in the total work of redemption. "I rejoice in the sufferings I bear for your sake, and what is lacking of the sufferings of Christ, I fill up in my flesh for his body, which is the Church" (Col 1:24). Through this sharing of his work, our Lord has made an admirable contribution to the bonds of love that unite the members of the family of God. If we never had to depend upon this family, nor they upon us, we would forget one another. By establishing this constant communication of mutual aid between the different parts of the Community, love is greatly fostered. We become grateful for the wonderful household of saints to which we belong and we resolve to become involved in all its activities. Because of the greatness of their love, some members deserve our attention more than others. Like a little child turning to a big brother or an elder sister, we should go without hesitation to the great saints to seek their help in time of need.

XXI

The Faith of the Blessed Virgin Mary

The saint closest to Christ in every way is Mary, the Blessed Mother. As the brethren of Christ, all of us are related to Mary most intimately. Being the eldest daughter of the Church, Mary is our "big sister" who is so much wiser, better and more experienced than we are. As the mother of Jesus, she is the mother of that life of Christ which dwells within everyone who is in the state of grace. In addition to all this, we are related to Mary as members of the same human family. It is through her that the whole human race is related by flesh and blood to the Son of God. It was a piece of her human flesh that became the divine flesh of the God-man and it was the humanity received from her that paid the price of our redemption on Good Friday, arose gloriously and immortal on Easter Sunday and ascended triumphantly on Ascension Thursday, and that now sits at the right hand of God in heaven, equal to the heavenly Father in all things.

Jesus Christ will always be the perfect model of sanctity for all Christians. Before the Incarnation, Mary was the first example for the human race; but once Christ was conceived, he became the supreme representative of all mankind. Nevertheless, there were certain accidental qualities which a divine Person could not assume: the condition of being created and redeemed; the human virtues of faith and hope, and that condition of life which sums up all the others —femininity. In all these Mary is our supreme model at the Incarnation, on Calvary, at Pentecost, today in heaven and during the Mass. In each of these mysteries of our redemption, Mary plays a secondary role to that of Christ, but nevertheless, an essential role. In the particular plan of salvation chosen by God, her activity is necessary if the plan is to reach a successful conclusion. Just as God's first plan depended upon the free consent of Adam, so the Incarnation of Christ depends upon the free consent of Mary. It would be contrary to all nature and reason for God to have compelled Mary, against her will, to be the mother of Christ. What would have happened if she had said "no," we can only conjecture, but we can presume that God would have found another way to save us. Thanks be to God, Mary said "yes," and for this we should always be grateful.

The activity of Mary in the work of Christ's redemption centers around her faith and love. At the Incarnation, she was asked to consent to his life; on Calvary, she had to consent to his death. Actually, the two consents were but one act of loving faith, since her blind assent to God's will at the Annunciation carried with it a virtual consent to the whole work of salvation. Like Mary, we also have to work in the darkness of faith throughout our life on earth; therefore a study of how she acted in times of crisis will help us to make the right decisions when our faith and love are put to the test. If we will consent wholeheartedly to each of God's calls of grace, as did Mary at the Annunciation, we too will experience an incarnation of the life of Christ within us. If we accept our role of suffering as Mary accepted her pain on Calvary, we will have a share in Christ's work of redemption. "What is lacking of the sufferings of Christ I fill up in my flesh for his body, which is the Church" (Col 1:24).

The first crisis of which we are aware in the life of Mary occurred at the Annunciation. "When she heard (the Angel) she was troubled at his word and kept pondering what manner of greeting this might be" (Lk 1:29). "How shall this happen, since I do not know man?" (Lk 1:34). Having been told what God wanted of her, it still required an heroic act of faith on her part to make the plunge into the vast, unknown territory of divine motherhood. Nevertheless, she wholeheartedly accepted everything that God willed for her. "Behold the handmaid of the Lord, be it done to me according to thy word" (Lk 1:38). At this crucial moment in the history of salvation, it is Mary's act of faith that wins the victory over Satan and sin. "Blessed is she who has believed, because the things promised her by the Lord shall be accomplished" (Lk 1:45). In abandoning herself completely to God, Mary's faith and love took a tremendous step forward; the capacity of her soul for grace was enlarged and the Lord filled it to overflowing. Having received so much from the Lord, her first thought is to share it with others. Being filled herself with Christ, she gives him to others whenever she gives herself. "How have I deserved that the mother of my Lord should come to me," St. Elizabeth asked at the time of the Visitation (Lk 1:43). As Mary brought the invisible Christ to Elizabeth and Zachary, she was vividly aware of her own lowliness, along with the greatness of her new vocation. "My soul magnifies the Lord and my spirit rejoices in God my Savior; because he has regarded the lowliness of his handmaid; for behold, henceforth all generations shall call me blessed; because he who is mighty has done great things for me and holy is his name" (Lk 1:46-49).

Following her example, we must allow ourselves to be so filled with Christ that we, too, will become Christ-bearers.

All of Christian tradition insists that Mary was the virginal mother of Christ. Just as she was preserved from original sin by her Immaculate Conception, so she was preserved from the two penalties announced in Genesis, the pains of childbirth and the corruption of the tomb (Gn 3:16-19). She shared in the work of redemption through the acts of faith which were required of her during the Nativity and Infancy of Christ. It had been clearly revealed to her that her son was the Son of the Most High, despite all outward appearances to the contrary. Again and again she had to make acts of blind faith in the Word of God that gave testimony to his divinity. Each time her faith was tested, she responded wholeheartedly to God's grace.

From the beginning, Mary knew that Jesus was the "Savior" destined to "save his people from their sins" (Mt 1:21). At the Presentation, Simeon made plain to her two facts: (1) "This child is destined for the fall and the rise of many in Israel and for a sign that shall be contradicted; (2) thy own soul a sword shall pierce" (Lk 2:34-35). Still living in the darkness of faith, she did not know all that this might entail; but it was clear that there would be much suffering. Pain is contrary to our human nature and no mother could naturally desire this vocation for either her child or herself. St. Luke says that Mary and Joseph were astonished at what they heard, but there was no refusal to accept God's will. Making the necessary effort, Mary rose above the desires of her natural motherhood and made a new step of faith into the unknown future.

Another act of faith was required when they found the Christ-child in the temple. "They did not understand the word that he spoke to them" (Lk 2:50). Again, working in the dark, Mary conformed her will to the will of God. Her natural motherly possessiveness of Jesus had to be made subservient to his "Father's business" (Lk 2:49). We can only guess at the effort required to rise to this new relationship. This would not be the only time that Christ would ask her to take a place second to others. At Cana she is told, "What is this to me and to you, my hour has not yet come" (Jn 2:4). During his public life, our Lord makes answer to the woman who praised his mother, "Rather, blessed are they who hear the word of God and keep it" (Lk 11:28). Once she tried to interrupt him during a busy day with the disciples. "Behold, thy mother and thy brethren are outside, seeking thee." Jesus answered, "Who are my mother and my brethren?" And stretching forth his hands toward his disciples, he said, "Behold my mother and my brethren" (Mt 12:47-49). Mary humbly submitted to her secondary role during the public life of Christ. She had no claims upon him when it was a matter of his proclaiming the good news of salvation. Because she was willing to follow God's will, Mary has become the model of all those, especially mothers, who must sacrifice their natural possessiveness on one level in order to rise to a new height of maturity and sanctity. "His mother kept all these things carefully in her heart" (Lk 2:51).

Mary's vocation was that of a mother, not a priest or an apostle. She is not given the commission to go out and preach the Gospel to all nations, nor the power to forgive sins or to change bread and wine into the Body and Blood of Christ. Nevertheless, she can help all those who are called to be priests and apostles. Her vocation is very feminine and truly motherly; it is an interior mission of prayer and suffering. She is not permitted near Christ during the public life of preaching, but we find her very close to him at the two key moments of his life on earth—his Incarnation and his Death. At the Conception and Birth of Christ, she is to the God-man everything a mother is supposed to be. On Calvary, through her union with Christ in his sufferings, she offers to the heavenly Father her faith and hope, her love as a mother and a woman, and unites these to the supreme offering of love made by Christ. Each time that the Sacrifice of Calvary is renewed in the Mass, these elements of Mary's sacrifice are integrated into Christ's and our sacrifice. Christ will always be our supreme model in love, but Mary is indeed the supreme model of faith and hope.

As Christ's mother, she willingly offered her Son on Calvary for the redemption of the world. Just as this was the crowning act of love on the part of Christ, so it was the greatest of all the acts of faith, hope and charity which Mary was ever asked to make. By co-operating with Jesus in the salvation of the world, she acquired a new title as mother of mankind. Christ is the new Adam and Mary becomes the new Eve of the redeemed human race. Mary's spiritual motherhood of all those who belong to Christ is a type of that supernatural motherhood which the Church, the Mystical Body of Christ, enjoys over us. The Church began only with the death of Christ; therefore, Mary anticipates the Church. At the Annunciation and on Calvary, the Church was hidden in Mary. She experienced in advance all that the new people of God would experience later. "Woman, behold thy son." Then Jesus says to all those disciples whom he loves, "Behold thy mother" (Jn 19:27).

On Pentecost, Mary once again assumes the hidden role Christ asked her to accept during his public life. She remains in the background, humbly subject to the authority of Christ in St. Peter and the Apostles, just as she had submitted herself earlier to her Son. However, this does not mean that she is no longer needed for the work of the Church. Mary still has the very important, feminine, motherly task of praying for the Church, especially all those active in the apostolate. During the remaining years of her earthly life and throughout the centuries since her Assumption, Mary's vocation is primarily that of intercessor before the throne of the heavenly Father. She is not alone today; the first Pentecost is re-enacted as the whole Communion of Saints unites its prayers with hers and with Christ's for a new Pentecost, a new day of grace. "All these with one mind continued steadfastly in prayer with the women and Mary, the Mother of Jesus, and with his brethren" (Acts 1:14).

By her Assumption, Mary has become the fulfillment of all that the Church ever hopes to attain. Her life of faith while on earth is the perfect model for our faith; likewise, her glorified body in heaven gives added reason to our own hope of resurrection. Beside the assurance of the Risen Body of Christ, we are given a further incentive to our hope for the third aeon in the doctrine of the Assumption. What has happened to the body of Mary will, also, occur with our bodies on the Last Day, if we have followed her example of heroic faith, hope and charity. The glorification of her body takes our faith another step toward completion, since we are concerned here with a human person and not a divine Person. There can be no doubt that God intends to glorify us just as he glorified Jesus, the God-man, and Mary, the first member of Christ's Church.

Meditation on the mysteries of our salvation as seen in Mary, can be a most fruitful source for our growth in grace. If we understand her vocation as the Mother of God, devotion to Mary will never lead us away from Christ but always to a closer union with him. She is in no way above him or equal to him, but rather totally subservient to him.

Her one desire for us in relation to her divine Son is expressed with beautiful simplicity in the words she spoke to the servants at Cana, "Do whatever he tells you" (Jn 2:5). Her power of intercession and mediation, like the whole Communion of Saints, has value only in and through Christ. "There is one God and one Mediator between God and men, himself man, Christ Jesus" (I Tim 2:5). She is not a second Christ, she is the mother of Christ, and all her value to the world and to God is found in her motherhood, both natural and spiritual. Because her vocation as mother is so similar to our vocation as a creature, we do well to learn all we can about her, ask her intercession and imitate her faith, hope and charity.

XXII

The Heroic Charity
of the Saints

Besides the Blessed Mother, everyone should have his or her favorite saints from both sexes. Frequently one will find in a saint of the opposite sex the necessary complement to his own personality. Getting to know this saint quite well will enable one to grow in natural maturity as well as sanctity. By studying the saint's life and especially his or her words, we can get to know the personality well enough to feel a truly intimate friendship for someone long since dead. It is important that we read those lives of the saints which are honestly written, giving both sides of the saint's temperament and character. Simply because the Church has canonized them does not mean they were always saints. Nearly all of them had evil tendencies that required great grace and heroic efforts on their part to transform into virtues. If we get a true picture of their struggle to attain sanctity, we receive immense consolation and encouragement in our own efforts and failures.

Every person is unique in the particular character and vocation given by God; therefore, it is a grave error to attempt a slavish imitation of any one of the saints. The only exception to this is our imitation of Jesus Christ, who as the God-man completely comprehends all the possible types of personality and sanctity that may be created. An attempt to pattern our lives exactly after that of a saint is especially dangerous if we do not have a clear and complete picture of that person. Even when the biographies or autobiographies are adequate and true, it is wrong to accept what they did as being also best for us. Religious should know the particular spirit of the founder of their order or congregation and try to maintain this same spirit. However, it is a mistake when religious try to follow their founder in every word and detail of his or her life.

For one thing, times and conditions have changed. It is reasonable to suppose that if the particular founder or foundress were living today, he or she would often act differently from what was done in another age. The world has advanced tremendously in the knowledge of revealed truth as well as nature. Simply because a man or woman was a great saint does not mean that this person made no mistakes during his life. It is necessary that we subject each of the words and actions of the saint to the principles of right reason as we know them today. If they appear valid, we should follow them. This is the way that we follow our friends on earth. Because we love someone very dearly does not make that person infallible. Only a childish, immature love is blind to the faults of the beloved. In our relationship with the great saints of the past, we must love and accept them in a mature way.

There is one area of their life where we can imitate the saints without hesitation and this is their love for God, their neighbors and themselves. We ought to study the heroic charity which these great friends of God achieved, so that we can gain inspiration and enlightenment for our own lives. Each of them developed this field of charity in a unique way, according to the specific vocation and personality given to them. By studying the manner in which these saints practiced charity, we will know better what God expects of us. We should try to find saints who had similar vocations to our own; likewise those who have lived near our time or in similar conditions of life. When we find a personality and temperament that strikes a responsive chord in our souls, then we have discovered a true friend in the full sense of the word.

In each of the saints we can discover a special charm. Besides their great charity, the thing most appealing in the saints is their simplicity. They are so honest and straightforward: free of masks and completely themselves. Because they were so open in their speech and manner of behavior, they usually made enemies who resented their directness. It makes interesting reading to see how the saints coped with their persecutors, either before or after their death. A delightful sense of humor will often be seen in the saints who refused to take themselves too seriously and also in the way our Lord dealt with those who opposed them. We all appreciate genuineness and sincerity and these qualities will never be lacking in any saint. His life is a straight line toward God, without any double-dealing or complexities. This simplicity will be noticed especially in their prayer-life. They realized that God was a real person, someone to whom they could speak directly and from the heart.

Their heroic charity gave them a familiarity and confidence with the Lord that served as a recompense for the many crosses they endured to attain sanctity. Although keenly aware of their own weakness and nothingness, they were very much aware of God's infinite goodness and deep love for them. Their humility and confidence in God gave a beautiful balance to their lives that enabled them to run swiftly along the path of perfection. Filled with great faith and hope, the saints were able to attain a wonderful peace and joy here upon earth. They vividly realized that God is all-powerful, all-wise and all-good. They had many proofs of God's infinite love for them. Putting all these ingredients together, they discovered a recipe for happiness right here in the second aeon. All of this is reflected in their faces, their eyes, their smile, their entire behavior. Most of all, it is seen in the serene confidence they have toward the future as well as the present. Those who are close to them will imbibe some of this same confidence, if they are open to God's grace. God proportions his goodness to the degree of our confidence in him. "If thou canst believe, all things are possible to those who believe" (Mk 9:23).

Another characteristic of the charity of the saints is seen in the immense desires they have. There is nothing small about anything they do, whether it is motivated by natural love or supernatural charity. They are never content with the lowest place in God's esteem, even though keenly aware of how little they deserve his love. Love has made them bold and daring in their desires. They have come to realize that he never resents these high aspirations, but takes great delight in giving his love in proportion to one's desires. They know that we can never ask too much of God; that we actually show honor to his infinity when we make these bold requests. Neither does the consciousness of their past sins hinder their high desires. They know that God's love is sufficient to take away all their sins as a drop of water might disappear in a flaming furnace.

The saint is not content merely to ask for great things for himself, he is just as desirous that these same things be shared by all his brethren. He has a deep consciousness of the needs of the whole human family—their problems become his problems. Love and sanctity are actually synonymous, therefore for the saint love of God and brethren are as natural and instinctive as breathing. They have in a real sense become all love, loving without measure or limit, loving even unto folly. In the eyes of many of their friends, they may appear foolish and impractical in the extremes to which their love will go. Without concern for human respect, they desire to love God and all of God's family as they have never been loved in the past. They endeavor to let no opportunity pass, no matter how small, when it is possible for them to be of service to God and others.

The heroic charity of the saints will be expressed by a great zeal for God's glory and for the spread of his Kingdom. Aflame with his love, they are never happy unless working in some way for his glory and the welfare of their neighbors. They tax their minds and imaginations to discover all the possible ways to carry out their great charity. Following the example of Christ when he washed the feet of the apostles, their whole life is one of humble service to their brethren, being willing to lay down their lives for the salvation of others. They desire God to be known, loved and served by all and they do all in their power to tell the world about the wonderful things of God. They suffer keenly when they see God's love despised, ignored or rejected. They are ever seeking generous souls who will give to God the love that he deserves and desires. "We have but the single day of this life in which to save souls and thus give proof to Jesus of our love. Let us therefore refuse him nothing. He so much wants our love" (St. Therese). Believing that love makes all things possible, the saints are never discouraged by their own weakness and smallness. Through faith and hope, they know that even their highest desires can be accomplished.

Charity, like faith and hope, is a supernatural gift of God. In order to receive so great a love, the saint must abandon his whole self to God. The writings of the saints find different ways to describe this complete surrender of their being to the love of God. It is sometimes called the "gift of oneself" to emphasize the freedom of choice that the saint offers in making available for God's use all the faculties and energies that have been given him. They may speak of themselves as victims of love, to express the total consecration of their life to God. Victimhood means that their gift of self is absolute, indeterminate, everlasting, constantly renewed and completely generous. This is sometimes expressed as abandonment to the will of God, to emphasize that they allow God to dispose of them as he chooses. They have endeavored to make their wills so completely attuned to the least inspiration of grace, that they respond instantly to every indication of God's will for them, and joyfully accept it, no matter how lowly or difficult may be the task assigned to them. If God so wills, they accept without hesitation the heaviest crosses, suffering intensely but patiently as did Christ, their model. That no conditions have been placed on their surrender, is proven by the selflessness of their lives. Their dedication to God is prudent, calm, humble, trustful, entire, courageous, persevering.

An interesting thing about the great saints is that it is often difficult to determine the particular temperament that was most natural to them. As a person grows toward the fullness of sanctity, he learns to develop all the unconscious powers of his character. Through cooperation with God's grace, the saint has succeeded in bringing to perfection all the different sides of his personality originally asleep in the depths of his soul. Just as in our Lord's life, we can see every possible temperament perfectly portrayed, so in a similar way we see a beautiful balance in the personality of the heroic saint. On different occasions, he will show forth, first one virtue and then another; but all of them are fused by charity into a marvelous simplicity. St. Thomas Aquinas defines peace as the tranquillity of order. This is the peace possessed by the saints.

At the same time, there is a wonderful variety among the saints. Each of them has developed his particular talents and personality to perfection and no two of them are alike. For this reason, we find ourselves attracted at times more to one saint than to another. Often in our devotion we pass from one saint to another; a saint that was a great inspiration to us in youth will not necessarily be the model we follow in mature adulthood. Divine providence has mercifully given us this almost unlimited choice, so that there will be a saint for every occasion. If we come to know them well, we will find in their example the inspiration to help us attain the particular manifestation of heroic charity that God desires for us. If God were willing to help them reach the heights of love that they did, we can believe and hope that he will do the same for us.

XXIII

Living with Christ through the Liturgical Year

In his loving kindness, God has given us a most beautiful way to express our love for him in the second aeon. The liturgy of the Mass, as celebrated in the different feasts of the liturgical year, relives the whole history of salvation. By means of the historical dimension of the liturgy, the events of the past, especially the life of Christ, are made present as we celebrate Christmas, Epiphany, Holy Week, Easter and Ascension. "As often as you shall eat this bread and drink the cup, you proclaim the death of the Lord, until he comes" (I Cor 11:26). At the same time, the liturgy anticipates the events yet to come by means of the eschatological or future dimension. During Mass, time ceases to exist and we live for a while in the eternal "now" where the past, present and future are all one. We make contact with those events of long ago which brought us our salvation. At the same time, we live for a few moments in the third aeon which we hope to attain on the Last Day. This life of the future is experienced behind the veil of faith, but nevertheless, it is an actual experience for those who have the grace.

The history of salvation, past and future, is experienced

in two ways during the liturgy of the Mass—through the Liturgy of the Word and the Liturgy of the Eucharist. In the Liturgy of the Word, our contact with the past and future is made through the words of Sacred Scripture. During the Liturgy of the Eucharist, the symbols of the consecrated bread and wine are used to unite us to the living Christ, past, present and future. It is impossible for our limited minds and hearts to have a satisfactory experience with all these events within the confines of one Mass. Therefore, the Church has wisely stretched the celebration of the history of salvation over the course of the whole liturgical year. We have more time now to dwell on these great events and we find a freshness and variety in our liturgical celebrations which adds to our appreciation and enjoyment.

What we read and hear in Sacred Scripture tells us something of the actual events of past history. By means of grace-life, these events are made present. In addition, the Scripture contains a message concerning the future life in the Kingdom of God. What God did in the past indicates what he intends to do in the present and the future, but not in exactly the same way. The Christian interpretation of history is not a closed circle but a spiral movement that mounts ever higher and higher until it attains its goal in the third aeon. Again and again we come back to a similar situation, but always from a higher point of view. The words of Scripture describe this whole journey up the spiral ladder to the life of everlasting union with God. What is said in the Bible is applicable to life at any stage of growth from the beginning to the completion of the Kingdom on the Last Day. When in the domain of Scripture, time disappears and we consider things from the point of view of eternity.

What is true of the reading of Sacred Scripture in general, is especially true when it is proclaimed at Mass during the Liturgy of the Word. All its dimensions come to life as we listen to the Word of God spoken and explained through the liturgy. In Advent, we are back with the prophets and other people of the Old Testament, longing for the coming of Christ. At the same time, we are preparing for his coming now in the Eucharist and later on the Last Day. Everything that Isaia and the Baptist said to prepare the people for the first coming of Christ can be applied during the present Advent to our preprations for his coming in the Mass and for his final coming at the end of time. As we participate in Advent each year, we must try to keep all three dimensions in mind. To enjoy the full experience of liturgical living, we need the help of the whole community. Each member of the congregation is given a particular task to perform, and it is only when everyone cooperates that we attain the fullness of a liturgical celebration.

During the Easter cycle, we renew the events of our redemption as first experienced by Jesus Christ two thousand years ago. Through our devout participation in the liturgy of Holy Week and the Paschal Season, these events of the past are made present so that we can share in them. If we are in tune with the liturgy, we will experience a real death in our life of sin and evil attachments during Lent and Holy Week. During the great service of the Easter Vigil we will go through a personal resurrection of grace in the solemn proclamation of Christ's resurrection. We will also take part by anticipation in the future events of our own death and the glorious resurrection from the dead. These events happen to us through faith, but this does not mean that it is unreal. Only those can understand who have actually tasted the joy and happiness of an encounter with the living Christ during a liturgical celebration.

On the feast of the Ascension, we commemorate the

first Ascension of Christ into heaven and we celebrate our own ascension today by means of grace into the bosom of the heavenly Father; most of all, we anticipate the glorious ascension of the whole human race on the Last Day. Similarly, at Pentecost we renew the first Descent of the Holy Spirit, we participate in a new descent of the Spirit by means of grace, and we experience something of the encounter with the Holy Spirit that will take place on the Last Day.

Those who carry out liturgical services in the proper way will never envy the people of Christ's time, nor those who will still be alive on the Last Day. Through faith, they are able to share in the same joys and blessings as did the apostles on the first Easter and Pentecost and as will those who are alive at the final coming of Christ. There is always the veil of faith hiding from our eyes a direct vision of these events of liturgy, but as we grow in faith, year by year, this blindness will mean less and less. There are other ways to experience an encounter of love with the living Christ. We should look forward with expectation to the beatific vision in heaven and the renewed creation of the Last Day; nevertheless, we can appreciate the special value of a life of faith and hope. During this present aeon we love God in a way that after death we will never again have the opportunity to do. While on earth, we are able to prove our love for God by loving him blindly through acts of faith. This heroism will no longer be possible in heaven or in the third aeon. If we value our present opportunities, we will make the most of them as long as God sees fit to leave us upon earth. Faith and hope are essential to an encounter with Christ during liturgy; on the other hand, the more real experience we have in liturgical living, the stronger will become our faith and hope.

During the Liturgy of the Eucharist, we actually celebrate what has just been proclaimed and explained in the Scripture lessons and homily. Through the symbols of bread and wine our life is united to the life of the Blessed Trinity; the Holy Spirit unites us to Christ and Christ presents us to the Father. The Father is pleased with the gifts which Christ presents to him and desires to show his joy by sharing with us the gift that is closest to his heart, the Body and Blood of his Son. At the banquet table of the Lord, we are privileged to partake of this food, and through the symbolism of eating we are united with Christ and through Christ with the Father, the Spirit, and all our brethren.

There is an infinite variety in the offering and eating of the Body and Blood of Christ. The Eucharist which we celebrate and receive on Christmas should be different from the one at Ascension or Pentecost. According to the spirit of each season and feast, we offer and receive Christ. In addition, the Eucharist is celebrated each year according to the disposition of the people who take part in it. The more we grow in grace, the more we can unite ourselves to Christ in the various events of his life. The better the whole community participates in the liturgical service, the greater will be their individual union with Christ. As the people of God in a particular parish come to understand the deeper meaning of the liturgy, the Eucharistic celebrations will become new and fresh experiences for everyone participating. We live in God's world and God's time during liturgy, and there is no end to the possibilities of encounter.

Those who lack faith see only the external symbols which conceal the internal grace. "Seeing, they may see but not perceive; and hearing, they may hear but not understand" (Mk 4:12). If the music, vestments and gestures are beautiful, those merely watching the spectacle may experience a certain elevation of their spirits. They might find themselves inspired by a beautiful liturgical ceremony, so that they can pray more reverently and fervently while the liturgy is being performed in their presence. However, this is only the shell or the rind; the real fruit of the liturgy is hidden from these people and is reserved for those who can participate in the service with an intelligent and genuine faith and hope. It is unfortunate that so many Christians lack the understanding and faith needed to experience the real encounters with Christ that are available in the liturgy.

The language of the liturgy is the language of love. Only those who have had satisfying experiences of love are able to enter into the full action of a liturgical celebration. The Church's liturgy is so rich that everyone can derive some benefit from it, provided he have good will. However, the more real love, both natural and supernatural, that exists in our hearts, the more capable we will be of entering into the intensity of union available to us at every Mass. Besides love, there is need of an appreciation of the meaning of the particular feast. This requires study or explanation as well as time for reflection. For many centuries, the Church has very wisely expected religious and other devout people to prepare for their participation in the liturgy by a period of meditation. On the Sundays and greater feasts, this preparation should begin the previous night by means of a Bible Service, either publicly or privately. For the greatest of all liturgical celebrations, the Easter Vigil Service, all of Lent and especially Holy Week, are meant to be a preparation. Even our bodies need to be prepared for liturgy by the proper rest and relaxation, so that we can give our whole selves to the encounter with Christ.

In the twenty-first chapter of St. John's Gospel, there is a beautiful scene in the life of the apostles after the Resurrection of Christ. This Scripture passage describes the experience of love that we should have at the beginning of each day as we celebrate the Eucharistic liturgy. The apostles had spent the whole night on the lake without catching any fish. Early in the morning, weary and discouraged, they are rowing back to shore. A voice speaks to them across the water, "Have you any fish?" "No," they reply. "Cast the net to the right of the boat and you will find them." They cast, therefore, and were unable to draw it up for the great number of fish it contained. The disciple whom Jesus loved, said, "It is the Lord!"

St. Gregory the Great, in his description of this Gospel passage, tells us that Peter's boat represents the Church and the lake illustrates the ups and downs of life in this second aeon. In the darkness of the early morning, our Blessed Lord directs our work in the apostolate from the shore of the third aeon. If we obey him, we will catch such a number of fish that the boat cannot contain them; but we will have to row to shore, dragging the net after us. There on the shore, in the dawn of a new day, stands our Lord. When, therefore, they had landed, they saw a fire ready and fish laid upon it and bread. "Come and breakfast," he invited them, just as he invites us to the Eucharist each morning. And none of those reclining dared ask him, "Who art thou?" knowing it was the Lord. And Jesus came and took bread and gave it to them and likewise the fish. When, therefore, they had breakfasted, Jesus said to Simon Peter, "Simon, son of John, dost thou love me?" He said to him, "Yes, Lord, thou knowest that I love thee." He said to him, "Feed my lambs."